halloween

101 frightfully fun ideas

Better Homes and Gardens® Books
Des Moines, Iowa

Better Homes and Gardens® Books
An imprint of Meredith® Books

Halloween: 101 Frightfully Fun Ideas
Editor: Carol Field Dahlstrom
Technical Editor: Susan M. Banker
Graphic Designer: Angela Haupert Hoogensen
Copy Chief: Catherine Hamrick
Copy and Production Editor: Terri Fredrickson
Book Production Managers: Pam Kvitne,
    Marjorie J. Schenkelberg
Contributing Copy Editor: Carol Boker
Contributing Proofreaders: Becky Danley,
    Diane Doro, Mary Duerson, Colleen Johnson,
    Sheila Mauck, Lisa Stone
Photographers: Andy Lyons Cameraworks,
    Hopkins Associates, Peter Krumhardt, Scott Little
Technical Illustrator: Chris Neubauer Graphics, Inc.
Electronic Production Coordinator: Paula Forest
Editorial and Design Assistants: Judy Bailey,
    Mary Lee Gavin, Karen Schirm

Meredith® Books
Editor in Chief: James D. Blume
Design Director: Matt Strelecki
Managing Editor: Gregory H. Kayko

Director, Retail Sales and Marketing: Terry Unsworth
Director, Sales, Special Markets: Rita McMullen
Director, Sales, Premiums: Michael A. Peterson
Director, Sales, Retail: Tom Wierzbicki
Director, Sales, Home & Garden Centers: Ray Wolf
Director, Book Marketing: Brad Elmitt
Director, Operations: George A. Susral
Director, Production: Douglas M. Johnston

Vice President, General Manager: Jamie L. Martin

Better Homes and Gardens® Magazine
Editor in Chief: Jean LemMon
Executive Food Editor: Nancy Byal

Meredith Publishing Group
President, Publishing Group: Christopher M. Little
Vice President, Consumer Marketing & Interactive
    Media: Hal Oringer

Meredith Corporation
Chairman and Chief Executive Officer: William T. Kerr

Chairman of the Executive Committee: E. T. Meredith III

All of us at Better Homes and Gardens® Books are dedicated to providing you with information and ideas to create beautiful and useful projects. We welcome your comments and suggestions. Write to us at: Better Homes and Gardens Books, Crafts Editorial Department, 1716 Locust St., Des Moines, IA 50309-3023.

If you would like to purchase any of our books, check wherever quality books are sold. Visit our website at bhg.com or bhgbooks.com.

Cover Photograph: Andy Lyons Cameraworks

Photo Styling Assistant: Donna Chesnut

Our seal assures you that every recipe in *Halloween: 101 Frightfully Fun Ideas* has been tested in the Better Homes and Gardens® Test Kitchen. This means that each recipe is practical and reliable, and meets our high standards of taste appeal. We guarantee your satisfaction with this book for as long as you own it.

halloween

Get ready for tricks and treats, fun and fright—it's Halloween! What better time to plan a party, trim the haunted halls, and enjoy delicious treats than on the eeriest, silliest, spookiest night of the year.

Halloween is a wonderful time to get together with special friends and family members. Whether for a merrymaking trick-or-treat outing or a masquerade party at home, we'll help you celebrate in style.

Come along as we share Halloween ideas to transform your home into a haunted house or simply add a festive touch here and there. From unforgettable pumpkins to centerpieces and lighting ideas, your house will be the talk of the neighborhood.

If a party is in the plans, you'll enjoy recipes for can't-resist snack mixes, tempting drink concoctions, sandwiches any monster will love, and sweets so yummy you'll wish Halloween came every month. We'll even show you some great invitations you can make and decorations to make party goers giggle.

To encourage imaginations to soar, there are oh-so-clever costume ideas. No matter if you have just minutes or an entire weekend to devote, you'll find a costume that will be a treat to wear.

We hope you enjoy all of the creative ideas in this book and that they inspire you to put a little more spirit in the holiday. Happy Halloween!

Carol Field Dahlstrom

contents

It's spooky!
It's creepy! It's
nothing but FUN!
Come along if
you dare...
the ghostly gala
has begun!

chapter 1

just pumpkins

**All dressed up and
ready to glow**

Creatively carved
or trimmed to last
for weeks, we'll
show you fun new
ways to decorate
pumpkins—the
favorite trim at
Halloween time.

chapter 2

tricks 'n' treats

**Goodies you'll
want to concoct**

Gather up delicious
recipes everyone
will love, along with
clever containers
to make and give
to all the special
trick-or-treaters at
your door.

just

All dressed up
and ready to glow

pumpkins

the crow's hideout

Ready for Halloween mischief, these artificial birds perched on the pumpkin-turned-birdhouse retreat appear to be real. Great for a centerpiece or last-minute trick-or-treat greeter, this quick pumpkin idea offers something to crow about.

supplies

Pumpkin
Knife, drill and large drill bit, or small, round cookie cutter
5-inch-long piece of ¼-inch dowel
Pencil sharpener
Paintbrush
Acrylic paints in black and white
3 artificial crows
Scissors; ruler
White paper
Tracing paper
Round pencil
Black marker
Medium-gauge wire; nail
Raffia or straw

what to do

1 Cut a round circle in the pumpkin on the lower half as shown, *opposite.* You can use a knife, a drill and bit, or a small, round cookie cutter.

2 Sharpen one end of the dowel in a pencil sharpener. Paint the dowel black and let it dry. Add white dots by dipping the handle end of a paintbrush into paint and dotting onto the dowel. Let dry. Insert the sharp end of the dowel just below the cutout. Attach a crow to the perch. Firmly press the wire feet of the remaining crows into the pumpkin top where desired.

3 To make a "Happy Halloween" sign, cut a 5×1⅝-inch piece from white paper. Trace the lettering, *below,* onto tracing paper. Place the traced pattern under white paper and hold up to a window for light. Use a black marker to copy the lettering. Outline the paper edges with marker. Poke two small holes in the top of the sign as shown, *opposite.* Cut a 5-inch length of wire. Curl it by wrapping around a pencil. Push the ends of the wire into the holes in the sign and twist to secure. Insert the nail into the pumpkin to hang the sign. Fill the drilled hole with raffia or straw.

SIGN PATTERN

pumpkin pizzazz

Small pumpkins get big applause with simple-to-do techniques. The pumpkin, opposite, has Halloween words spelled out in alphabet macaroni and is accented with metallic paints.

The star version, below, becomes a dazzling delight covered with glistening stars of all colors.

spell-cast pumpkin

supplies

Pumpkin
Alphabet macaroni
Paintbrush
Glossy decoupage medium
Acrylic metallic paints in copper, green, purple, gold, or other desired colors
Pencil with round-tip eraser

what to do

1 Decide what words or phrases to add to the pumpkin. Find the letters in the alphabet macaroni to spell out your selection. Use the paintbrush to add a 1/8-inch-thick line of decoupage medium on the pumpkin where you want to add the macaroni. Place the macaroni letters on the decoupage medium, spelling out the Halloween words or phrases of choice. Continue adding selections until you like how it looks. Let the decoupage medium dry.

2 To add color to the macaroni letters, paint the top surfaces only, using very little metallic paint. Use only one color on the entire word or phrase so it stands out as a unit. Let the paint dry.

3 To add dots between the words, dip the eraser end of the pencil into copper paint. Carefully dot the paint onto the surface of the pumpkin where desired. Let the paint dry.

star-struck pumpkin

supplies

Star-shaped gems
Pumpkin
Silicone adhesive

what to do

1 Place all of the stars right side up so the colors can be seen. Decide how closely you want the stars placed.

2 Put a dab of silicone adhesive on the back of each star and press into place on the pumpkin. Let the glue dry.

This friendly ghost, peeking from his pumpkin home, is fun to make from lightweight clay. With a few bright details, this clever pumpkin becomes the center of attention at your Halloween party.

spooky surprise

supplies

Small pumpkin
Knife
Spoon
Four 8-inch-long
  pieces of ¼-inch
  dowel
Pencil sharpener
Acrylic paints in
  lime green and
  purple
Paintbrush
White Crayola®
  Model Magic®
  clay
2 small black
  beads
1 large black
  bead
Toothpicks
Shredded colored
  paper

what to do

1 Cut the pumpkin in half horizontally, keeping the cut line as smooth as possible. Clean out the inside by scraping it with a spoon.

2 Sharpen both ends of the dowels in a pencil sharpener, for easy insertion into the pumpkin. Paint two dowel pieces lime green and the remaining two purple. Let the paint dry. Add dots on each dowel by dipping the handle end of the paintbrush into paint and dotting onto the dowel surfaces. Let the paint dry. Paint the pumpkin stem purple. Let dry. Add green dots. Let dry. Insert the dowels into the bottom half of the pumpkin, then place the pumpkin top on by firmly pressing it onto the dowels.

3 To create the ghost, take a portion of clay suitable for the size of your pumpkin. Knead the clay until it is smooth. Shape the clay into an oblong smooth piece. Gently twist the top portion to create a ghostly head. Shape arms from small pieces of dough. Position the arms onto the ghost's body and press into place. Form the bottom of the ghost to fit inside the pumpkin.

4 Use the photograph, *below,* as a guide to make the eyes and mouth. Press the black beads into the face using a toothpick. Press toothpicks into the bottom of the pumpkin. Position the ghost over the toothpicks and press into place.

5 Add shredded paper around the pumpkin.

silver swirl pumpkin

Long after the jack-o'-lantern candles are blown out, this silver-laden pumpkin will shine on. Use it as a beautiful centerpiece or front porch decoration all autumn long perched on a bed of leaves or sitting all by itself. When the time comes to toss out the pumpkin, the solder swirls can be pulled out and saved to use year after year.

supplies
Lead-free solder in desired thicknesses
Wire cutter
Needle-nose pliers
Ice pick
Pumpkin

what to do

1 Using the wire cutter, cut 2- to 8-inch lengths from the solder. Approximately 50 pieces will be needed to trim a medium-size pumpkin like the one shown, *opposite*.

2 Using the photographs, *opposite* and *right,* as guides, twist the solder lengths into desired shapes. Use a needle-nose pliers to start bending the end of the solder into a small loop. You can bend the solder

lengths into coils, S-shapes, zigzags, or whatever you wish. Leave an inch at the end of the solder to bend perpendicular to the shape. This end of the solder will poke into the pumpkin to hold the solder shape in place.

3 Use an ice pick to poke holes in the pumpkin, approximately 3 to 5 inches apart. Insert the bent ends of the solder shapes into the holes to secure.

4 To add a solder shape to the pumpkin stem, first poke a hole in the stem using an ice pick. Shape a length of wire as desired, leaving 1 inch at an end to insert into the stem. Push the solder into the pumpkin stem.

metal magic

Add a stylish twist to make any pumpkin stand out from the rest. Cut from copper foil, the leaves poke easily into a pumpkin top, opposite. The coordinating pair, left and below, can be made in minutes using eyelets and grommets.

copper-leafed pumpkin

supplies
Tracing paper
Pencil
Old scissors
36-gauge copper tooling foil
Dish towel
Pointed skewer
20-gauge copper wire
Knife
Pumpkin

what to do
1 Trace the leaf patterns, *right,* onto tracing paper. Cut out shapes. Draw around leaf shapes on copper tooling foil. Cut out leaf shapes.

2 To make the leaf veins, first place the leaves on a dish towel. Using the pattern as a guide, make vein impressions using a skewer.

3 Cut four 14-inch lengths of wire. Wrap the wire lengths around the skewer and remove. Pull apart as desired to make curlicues.

4 Cut two small slits, each about 1 inch long, next to the pumpkin stem. Insert one tip of each leaf into a slit. Shape leaves as desired.

5 Twist the ends of the wire spirals together and press into the pumpkin near where the leaves are inserted.

rings pumpkin

supplies
Pumpkin
Gold grommets
Spoon, if needed
Gold and copper eyelets

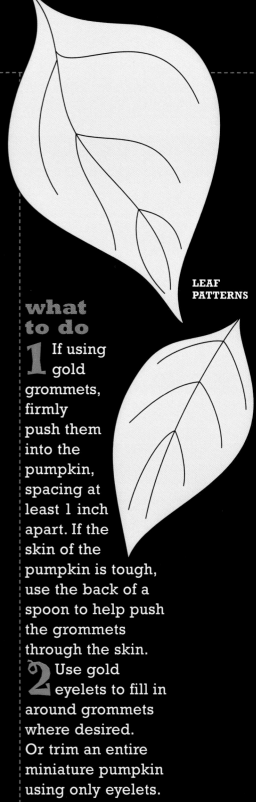

LEAF PATTERNS

what to do
1 If using gold grommets, firmly push them into the pumpkin, spacing at least 1 inch apart. If the skin of the pumpkin is tough, use the back of a spoon to help push the grommets through the skin.

2 Use gold eyelets to fill in around grommets where desired. Or trim an entire miniature pumpkin using only eyelets.

fallen leaves pumpkin

The colors of autumn are vividly enhanced by painting gathered leaves with bright metallic paints. A white pumpkin creates an unexpected, ghostlike backdrop for these favorite symbols of the fall season.

supplies
Dry leaves
Newspapers
Acrylic metallic paints in lime green, magenta, blue, and purple
Paintbrush
White pumpkin
Decoupage medium

what to do

1 Gather leaves in desired sizes and shapes. Make sure the leaves are dry but not brittle. Green leaves may curl and will not accept paint well.

2 Cover your work surface with newspapers. Paint the front sides of the leaves using metallic paints. Let the paint dry. Apply a second coat if needed. Let the paint dry. Turn the leaves over and paint the back, using the same color. Let the paint dry.

3 Paint the stem of the pumpkin using a desired color of metallic paint. Let the paint dry.

4 To attach the leaves to the top and sides of the pumpkin, coat the back of each leaf with decoupage medium. The leaves will not stay flat to the pumpkin, but will curl a bit. Press a leaf onto the pumpkin and paint over the front of the leaf with a coat of decoupage medium. Continue adding leaves in this manner until the desired look is achieved. Let it dry.

pretty patterned pumpkins

Using brushstrokes of metallic paint adds a contemporary touch to this beauty from the pumpkin patch. The details complementing the checkerboard pattern are made with easy-to-do dots and scribbles from a permanent marking pen.

Colorful plastic-coated wires seem to grow on the miniature pumpkin. Holes poked in the pumpkin anchor the vertical wires and separate wires twist around the stem.

check-it-out pumpkin

supplies
Acrylic metallic paints in teal and purple
1-inch flat paintbrush
Pumpkin
Metallic gold permanent marking pen
Pencil with round-tip eraser

what to do
1 Paint a teal checkerboard design on the pumpkin. To begin, start with the center of the pumpkin. Paint 1-inch squares around the center of the pumpkin. Continue making 1-inch checks over the entire pumpkin, alternating the positions as shown, *opposite*. Let the paint dry.

2 To add squiggles, draw them on top of the painted checkerboard as desired. Let it dry.

3 To add dots between the painted checks, dip the eraser end of a pencil into purple paint. Carefully dot on the surface where desired. Let the paint dry.

wire-wrapped pumpkin

supplies
Ice pick
Miniature pumpkin
Plastic-coated wire in desired colors
Old scissors

what to do
1 Using an ice pick, poke tiny holes at the top of each pumpkin crevice around the stem. Repeat on the bottom of the pumpkin.

2 Cut lengths of wire to reach from a top hole to a bottom hole, adding 2 inches. Bend over 1 inch at the end of a wire length. Push the short folded-over end into a hole at the top of the pumpkin. Gently pull the wire down the crevice of the pumpkin and firmly push the remaining wire end into the hole at the bottom. Repeat for each set of holes.

3 Cut a 3-inch piece of each color of wire. Twist together at one end. Wrap around stem as desired.

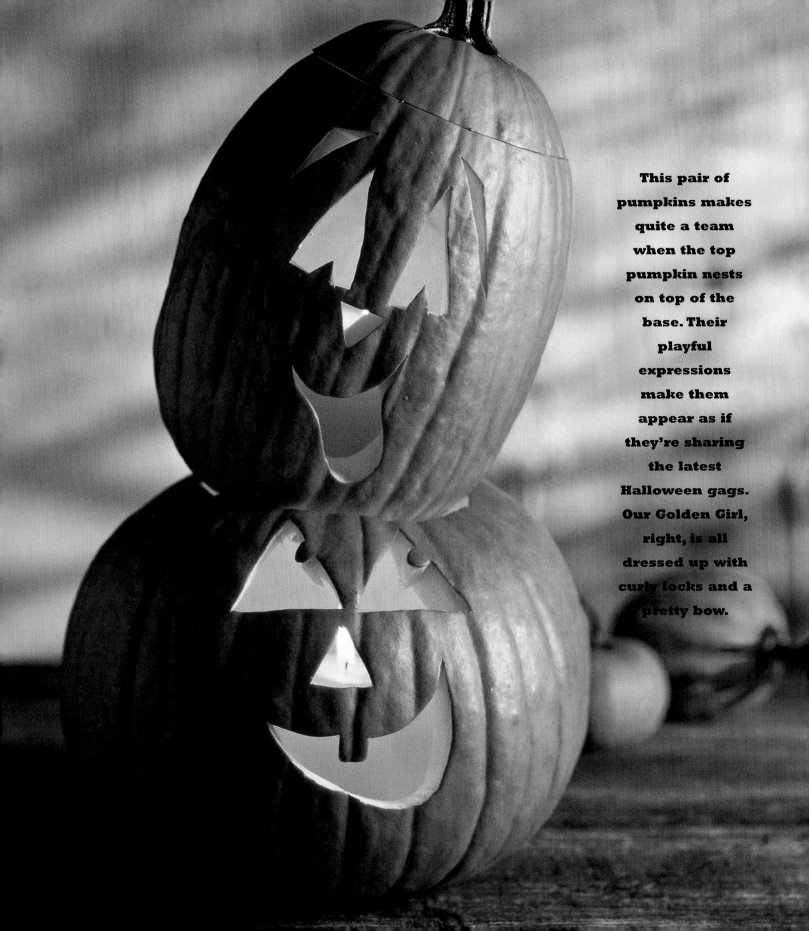

This pair of pumpkins makes quite a team when the top pumpkin nests on top of the base. Their playful expressions make them appear as if they're sharing the latest Halloween gags. Our Golden Girl, right, is all dressed up with curly locks and a pretty bow.

kooky characters

joking, jesting buddies

supplies
Knife
Large, round
  pumpkin
Large, tall
  pumpkin
Spoon
Fine permanent
  marking pen
Two votive
  candles
Match

what to do
1 Cut the top off each pumpkin and scoop out the insides using a spoon. Place the tall pumpkin on top of the round pumpkin. If necessary, enlarge the hole in the top of the round pumpkin so the tall one sits as shown.

2 Looking at the photograph, *opposite,* as a guide, draw faces on the pumpkins so that they look as if they're talking to each other. Cut out face shapes using a knife.

3 Place a candle in the round jack-o'-lantern and light. Position the tall pumpkin atop the round one. Place a candle in the tall jack-o'-lantern and light. Put on the lid. Be sure not to leave a burning candle unattended.

golden girl

supplies
Small, round
  pumpkin
Black
  eyelets
Black
  chenille stems
Round pencil,
  dowel, or skewer
Ice pick
Scissors
12-inch pieces of
  ribbon

what to do
1 Push an eyelet into the center of the pumpkin for the nose. Using the photograph, *right,* as a guide, make two triangular eyes and a smile using eyelets.

2 To make the hair, tightly wrap each chenille stem around a pencil, dowel, or skewer, and remove. Use an ice pick to make holes in the top of the

pumpkin where you want to add hair. Push the ends of the chenille stems into the holes. For bangs, cut chenille stems in half.

3 Tie two or three ribbons to the stem and allow to trail through the hair.

23

web-laden pumpkin

When the light falls upon this pumpkin, the glitter paint and faceted gems will sparkle with vibrant color. The web effect is easy to achieve by simply outlining the pumpkin crevices with a paint pen.

supplies
Pumpkin
Metallic paint pens in purple and gold
Gems in oval and rectangular shapes
Small metallic beads to match gems

what to do

1 To draw the spider web, use metallic purple paint pen. Start by following the vertical crevices in the pumpkin. Use the photographs, *opposite* and *right,* as guides, making the lines different lengths. When all of the vertical lines are painted, draw the horizontal lines, making them slightly scalloped and about 1 inch apart. Let the paint pen dry.

2 Decide where to add spiders. Place a small amount of metallic gold paint pen on the back of the gem for body. Use an oval gem for a large spider or a rectangular gem for a small spider. Place onto the pumpkin. If making a large spider, use a rectangular gem for the head. Place paint pen on the back of the gem and place it above the oval body. Outline the spiders using metallic gold paint pen. Press two bead eyes to the top of the head. Add paint pen legs and let dry.

3 Paint the stem of the pumpkin using metallic gold paint pen. Let the paint pen dry.

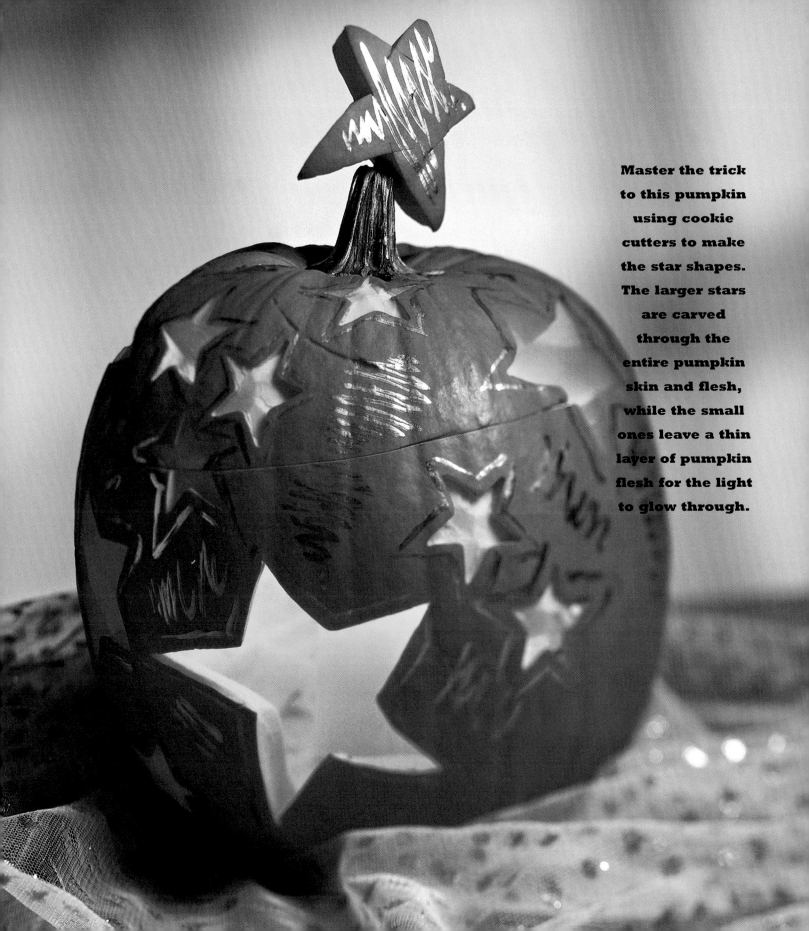

Master the trick to this pumpkin using cookie cutters to make the star shapes. The larger stars are carved through the entire pumpkin skin and flesh, while the small ones leave a thin layer of pumpkin flesh for the light to glow through.

glowing star pumpkin

supplies
Knife; spoon
Pumpkin
Star cookie
  cutters in
  desired sizes
Paring knife
Tracing paper
Metallic gold
  permanent
  marking pen
Toothpick
Candle
Match

what to do

1 Cut the top third off the pumpkin. Clean out the insides using a spoon.

2 Press a large cookie cutter into the pumpkin where you want the large stars cut out. Remove the cookie cutter and use a paring knife to carefully cut out the shapes. (If you do not have star cookie cutters, trace the patterns, *right*. Cut out patterns and trace star shapes on the pumpkin using gold marker. Use a knife to cut shapes from pumpkin.)

3 For the small stars, press the small star cookie cutter into the skin of the pumpkin, being careful not to pierce through the entire skin. Use a paring knife to remove the outer layer of skin, leaving a thin lining for the light to shine through.

4 Outline the star shapes with metallic gold marker. Use the marker to add squiggles between the star shapes, if desired.

5 Poke a toothpick into the bottom of one of the medium-size stars removed from the pumpkin. Color in the star shape using metallic gold marker. Color the raised areas of the stem using marker.

6 Poke a hole in the top of the stem. Insert the toothpick with the star on the end.

7 Place a candle inside the pumpkin, light the wick, and place the lid on the pumpkin. (Never leave a burning candle unattended.)

STAR PATTERNS

jester jack-o'-lantern

Any pumpkin, carved or fresh from the pumpkin patch, will look grand sitting upon this whimsical garden post. Trimmed with star-shape wood cutouts and beads on colored wires, the brightly painted post stands 4 feet tall.

supplies

**Pumpkin; spoon
Knife
Wood garden post
Saw; sandpaper
11×11-inch piece of
 ¾-inch-thick pine
Flower-shape
 wood clock face
 or 9-inch-square
 piece of ¾-inch-
 thick pine
Tack cloth
Acrylic paints in
 orange, black,
 yellow, purple,
 green, and white
Paintbrush; pencil
Tracing paper
Four 3-inch wood
 stars; five 1¾-inch
 wood stars
Twenty ¾-inch
 wood stars
Wood finial
Wood glue
Drill and drill bit
Six 2-inch-long
 wood screws
 with flat heads
Screwdriver
Assorted beads
Colored wire
Ice pick; toothpick
Candle; match**

what to do

1 Cut the top off the pumpkin in a zigzag pattern. Clean out the insides with a spoon. Carve a face on the pumpkin. Set it aside.

2 If desired, cut off the bottom of the garden post so it measures approximately 4 feet high. Sand any rough spots on the garden post, clock face, or remaining pine pieces. Remove any dust using a tack cloth.

3 Using the photograph, *right,* for ideas, paint the garden post. You can paint solid areas, checks, stripes, dots, or whatever you wish. To make the triangular shapes at the top of the

continued on page 31

29

STAND TOP PATTERN

FOLD

large stars, paint them green with a little yellow mixed in. Let the paint dry. Outline the lower edges of the triangles with yellow. For all other green painted areas, highlight with yellow while the green paint is wet. For the yellow areas, you can add touches of orange while the yellow paint is wet. When painting a black-and-white checked pattern, paint the entire area white first. When dry, add the black checks.

4 For the base, divide the top into four equal sections, drawing in the lines with a pencil. Paint two opposite corners orange and the remaining two black. Let the paint dry. Paint the edges with black and orange, creating a checked pattern. Let the paint dry.

5 For the wood piece that sits on the top of the post, use the wood clock face. If you prefer to cut a top piece from pine, trace the pattern, *opposite.* Cut out the pattern and trace around it on pine. Use a band saw to cut out the shape. Sand the edges if necessary. Paint the top solid purple and the edge with a black-and-white checked design. Let the paint dry. Add orange and green dots to the top edge, if desired. Let dry.

6 Paint the large and medium stars yellow. Dry-brush the edges using orange. Let the paint dry. Paint twelve of the small stars orange and the remaining stars yellow. Add yellow to the edges of the orange stars and orange to the edges of the yellow stars. Let dry.

7 Paint the finial as desired, using the photograph, *page 28,* for ideas. Let the paint dry.

8 Glue the large stars on the garden post as shown. Add a small star below each large one. Glue a medium star in each corner of the base piece. Glue small stars around the edge of the top piece, alternating orange and yellow stars. Let dry.

9 Drill a hole through the center of the round top piece. Drill a hole in the center of the top and bottom of the post. Drill a hole through the center of the base piece. Use screws to secure the base and top pieces to the post.

10 Tighten to secure. Thread desired beads onto wires. Put enough beads on to wrap around post where you want to add the beaded wires. Tie the wires in place. To curl the wire ends, wrap tightly around an ice pick.

11 Remove top from the pumpkin. Use an ice pick to poke a hole 1 inch deep in the stem of the pumpkin. Glue a toothpick in the hole. Place painted finial on toothpick. Add beaded wires and a wooden star to the topper.

12 Carefully place the pumpkin on stand, making sure it is balanced. Place a candle in the pumpkin and light it. Place on the lid. Be sure to never leave a burning candle unattended.

tricks

Goodies you'll want to concoct

'n' treats

monster mixes

A bewitching blend of sweet surprises will satisfy anyone's cravings for a snack. The painted jars are just right to hold a generous portion, and can serve as votive candleholders once the handles are removed. The instructions and mix recipe are on page 37. For more snack mixes and fun containers, turn the page.

PAINTED TOTE TRIO AND CREEPY CANDY MIX

OOKY 'N' SPOOKY TREAT CUPS
AND HONEY 'N' SPICE POPCORN

GHOULISH GOODY
JAR AND
GREMLIN GORP

BODY
BITS

OOKY THE CAT PATTERN

painted tote trio

supplies
Clear jars or glasses with a lip or threads
Tracing paper
Pencil
Scissors; tape
Glass paints in black, green, yellow, orange, purple, and white
Paintbrush; pencil with round-tip eraser
Chenille stems in black, orange, purple, and yellow

what to do
1 Wash and dry each jar or glass. Avoid touching the areas to be painted.

2 Trace the desired patterns, *page 38,* onto tracing paper. Cut out the patterns slightly beyond the drawn lines. Tape each pattern inside the jar where you wish to paint the design.

3 Paint the cat black, the pumpkin orange, or the swirl lime green (a mixture of green and yellow). Let the paint dry. Use the photographs on *pages 34–35* to paint on the details. If paints are layered, be sure to let the paint dry between coats. To add small dots, dip the handle end of a paintbrush into paint and dot onto the surface. For the larger dots, use the eraser end of a pencil.

4 To make a handle, use two contrasting chenille stems. Align ends and twist 1 inch from the ends. Bring long ends around jar top, one in front and one in back. Continue twisting chenille stems together, keeping them tight so they hold the jar. Twist the ends together to form the handle.

creepy candy mix

supplies
1 8-ounce bag candy-coated, peanut butter-flavor pieces
1 cup candy corn
1 10½-ounce bag miniature marshmallows

what to do
1 Toss the ingredients together in a mixing bowl. Makes about 7 cups.

ooky 'n' spooky treat cups

supplies
Clear plastic punch cups
Tracing paper
Pencil; scissors
Tape
Glass paints in black, green, yellow, and white
Paintbrush
Flat glass marbles in iridescent black and frosted clear or pale green
Silicone glue

what to do
1 Wash and dry the cups. Avoid touching the areas to be painted.

2 If painting the cat, trace the pattern onto tracing paper. Cut out slightly beyond the drawn lines.

continued on page 38

**PAINTED TOTE TRIO
CAT PATTERN**

**PAINTED TOTE TRIO
SWIRL PATTERN**

**PAINTED TOTE TRIO
PUMPKIN PATTERN**

Tape the pattern to the inside of the jar where you wish to paint the design. Place it low on the cup so the weight of the eyes does not tip the cup.

3 To make the cat cup, paint the cat black. Let the paint dry. Use the photograph on *page 36* to paint on the nose, mouth, and whisker details. To paint the marble eyes, mix a drop of green and yellow. Paint long ovals on the front sides of two frosted marbles. Let the paint dry. Paint smaller black ovals inside of the green ones. Let the paint dry. Glue the eyes in place and let dry.

4 To make the spider, glue two iridescent black marbles on the cup. Place them low enough so the cup does not tip. Let the glue dry. Paint on black legs. Let the paint dry.

honey 'n' spice popcorn

supplies
**10 cups popped corn (about ½ cup unpopped)
1 cup peanuts
¼ cup honey
3 tablespoons margarine
¼ teaspoon pumpkin pie spice**

what to do
1 Place popped corn and peanuts in a large roasting pan. In a small saucepan combine honey, margarine, and pumpkin pie spice. Heat and stir till margarine melts. Pour over popcorn and nuts, tossing to coat.

2 Bake in a 300° oven for 30 minutes, stirring about every 10 minutes. Transfer to a baking sheet; cool. Makes about 10 cups.

ghoulish goody jar

supplies
Jar with lip
Glass paints in black, green, yellow, orange, and white
Paintbrushes
Pencil with round-tip eraser
Black and white chenille stems

what to do
1 Wash and dry the jar. Avoid touching the areas to be painted. Paint black checks around the jar as shown on *page 36*, creating as many rows as the jar will allow. To create a row of lime green dots around the jar top, mix together a small amount of yellow and green paints. Dip the handle end of a paintbrush into the paint and dot on the surface, just below the lip. Let dry.

2 Paint orange dots where the checks meet, using the eraser end of a pencil. Let dry.

3 Add a white dot to the center of each check and a lime green dot to the center of each orange dot. Let dry.

4 For handle, align the ends of the chenille stems and twist to secure 1 inch from the ends. Bring the long ends around the jar top, one in front and one in back. Continue twisting the chenille stems together, keeping tight to hold the jar. Shape the handle and twist all ends together to secure.

gremlin gorp

supplies
1 6-ounce bag dried apricots, snipped, for dried skin (1 cup)
2 4½-ounce boxes of bite-size round crackers for witches' warts
1 6-ounce bag dried cranberries or cherries for dried drops of dragons' blood (1⅔ cups)
1 12-ounce jar dry-roasted peanuts for dried lizards' eyes (2⅓ cups)

what to do
1 Toss together in mixing bowl. Store in airtight bag or container up to 3 days. Makes 9 cups.

body bits

supplies
2½ cups coarsely crushed blue corn chips
1 cup corn nuts
1 cup raisins
1 cup pretzel sticks
1 cup canned shoestring potatoes
1 cup cheese sticks
½ cup shelled pistachio nuts or peanuts
Marshmallow ghost

what to do
1 Put the crushed corn chips, corn nuts, raisins, pretzel sticks, shoestring potatoes, cheese sticks, and nuts in a serving bowl. Stir. Garnish with a marshmallow ghost. Makes 8 cups.

2 To store, place mix in a plastic bag or container; cover tightly. Store in a cool, dry place for up to 2 weeks.

CAULDRON
CUPCAKES

dressed-up cupcakes

Cupcakes are always yummy to eat—even when they look like witch's cauldrons. This brewing concoction, in the scooped-out center of a cupcake, is made from pudding, gel frosting, and tiny candies. For more Halloween cupcake ideas, turn to page 42.

supplies for all cupcakes

Baked cupcakes
Spoon
Chocolate and vanilla frosting
Vanilla pudding or yogurt
Gel tube frosting
Small candies
String licorice
Paste food coloring
Candy corn
Fruit leather
Gumdrops
Edible glitter

cauldron cupcakes

what to do

1 Remove paper from a purchased or baked cupcake. Turn cupcake upside down; trim bottom if necessary to make cupcake stand straight.

2 Using a spoon, scoop out center, leaving ½ inch around the edges and about 1 inch on the bottom. Spread chocolate frosting on the sides and top of each cupcake.

3 Spoon the vanilla pudding or yogurt into the center of the cupcake. Decorate it with green gel tube frosting. Sprinkle the small candies onto the fillings. Push the ends of the licorice into opposite sides of the cupcake to make a handle.

monster cupcakes

what to do

1 Tint half of a can of vanilla frosting with green paste food coloring. Frost the top of one cupcake with white frosting. Remove the paper from another cupcake. Frost the entire cupcake with green frosting. Press top of green frosted cupcake into the top of the other paper-lined cupcake, leaving a gap in front (see the photograph on *page 42*). Place candy corn in the gap to form teeth.

2 Decorate cupcakes with small candies, string licorice, fruit leather, and gel frosting to complete the monster's face.

continued on page 42

SPIDER
CUPCAKES

spider cupcakes

what to do

1 If desired, tint vanilla frosting with orange and yellow paste food coloring. Frost cupcakes with white, orange, or yellow frosting.

MESSAGE
CUPCAKES

MONSTER
CUPCAKES

2 Push eight 2-inch pieces of red and/or black string licorice into a large black, orange, or yellow gumdrop, forming a spider, and press into the top of each frosted cupcake. Sprinkle the cupcakes with edible glitter.

message cupcakes

supplies
Tracing paper
Round pencil
Scissors
Crafting foam in purple and orange
Black permanent marker
Thick white crafts glue
5-inch pieces of wooden skewer
Chenille stems in purple, orange, and lime green
Paper punch

what to do

1 Trace the desired pattern, *right,* onto tracing paper. Cut out the pattern. Trace around the bat pattern on purple crafting foam or the jack-o'-lantern pattern on orange crafting foam. Cut out the shape.

2 Using the pattern for inspiration, draw in the features using permanent marker.

3 Glue a skewer to the back of the foam bat or pumpkin. Let the glue dry.

4 To add the green twist to the pumpkin, wrap a 4-inch piece of chenille stem around a pencil. Use a paper punch to add a hole near the stem in the pumpkin. Push one end of the chenille stem through the hole and twist to secure. To make the coils at the bottom, wrap an entire chenille stem around a pencil. Slip the skewer into the coil. Gently pull the coil apart until it covers 2 to 3 inches of the skewer. Push skewer into the center of the cupcake top.

MESSAGE CUPCAKES
BAT PATTERN

MESSAGE
CUPCAKES
JACK-O'-LANTERN
PATTERN

BOO!

HAPPY HALLOWEEN

cookie treats

Hats off to these chocolate temptations made from ice cream cones and purchased cookies. Each cone is filled with candy treats before it is attached to the base, making for a sweet surprise. The instructions follow on page 47. For more cookie treat ideas, turn the page.

CANDY-FILLED WITCHES' HATS

SUGAR COOKIE
FIX-UPS

46

candy-filled witches' hats

supplies

Self-sealing
  plastic bag
Can of chocolate
  frosting
Scissors
20 chocolate ice
  cream cones
Candy corn or
  assorted small
  candies
20 2- to 3-inch
  chocolate cookies
Waxed paper
Large green
  and yellow
  gumdrops

what to do

1 Fill a small
self-sealing
plastic bag with
some chocolate
frosting. Seal bag
and cut a very
small end off one
corner of the bag
and set aside.
Invert cone and
fill with about
2 tablespoons
candy corn or small
candies. Pipe some
frosting from bag
along bottom edge
of cone. Press a
cookie against
frosting. Carefully
invert right side up
onto waxed paper-
lined baking sheet.
2 Decorate
outside of cone
with small candies,
using additional
frosting as
necessary. Refill
frosting bag as
needed. If desired,
roll out large green
and yellow
gumdrops on a
sugared surface
until ⅛ inch thick.
Cut into ¼-inch
strips. Press green
strips around brim
of hat and cut
smaller pieces
from yellow strips
to make a buckle;
press onto hat.
Makes 20 hats.

sugar cookie fix-ups

supplies

Orange, yellow,
  and green paste
  food color
1 16-ounce can
  vanilla frosting
Purchased
  plain sugar
  cookies
Tubes of
  colored
  decorating
  frosting
  (red, green,
  yellow)
Small candies

what to do

1 Add food
coloring to
purchased vanilla
frosting, if desired,
to make orange,
yellow, and/or
green frosting.
Spread frosting on
sugar cookies and
decorate with tube
frosting and small
candies to make
jack-o'-lanterns,
ghosts, and
monsters. See
photos, *opposite*
and *below*, for
ideas.

spooky house with ghosts and ghouls

Constructing this haunted house provides an opportunity for the kids to join in. You supply all the ingredients and watch them search their imaginations to make the edible house even more scary.

supplies

1 16-ounce can chocolate frosting
Self-sealing plastic bags
16 honey graham cracker squares
4 chocolate graham cracker squares
1 clean 1-quart wax-coated paper milk carton
Serrated knife
7 black licorice twists
Small Halloween candy figures
Small candies
Green and yellow gel tube frosting
Orange and yellow decorating sugars

what to do

1 Spoon some chocolate frosting into a plastic bag. Snip off one small corner. Fill bag with more frosting as needed. Pipe frosting from bag onto one side of a honey graham cracker square and press against one side of milk carton, even with bottom. Repeat with two more squares to cover one side. Repeat on remaining three sides. Cut two honey graham cracker squares diagonally from both bottom corners to center of top to form two triangle pieces for top of house; trim to fit. Pipe frosting on one side of both pieces and press into place on carton. Pipe frosting on one side of two chocolate graham cracker squares and press onto top of milk carton for roof. Pipe frosting onto corners of house. Press licorice in place.

2 To form a door, halve a chocolate graham cracker square and use frosting to attach one rectangle to the front bottom of house. Saw two honey graham cracker squares into two rectangles each. Pipe frosting around door and attach three of the honey graham rectangles to form an entryway. Cut small pieces of chocolate crackers for shutters. Pipe frosting onto one side of shutters and Halloween candy figures. Press onto sides of house for windows.

3 Decorate with candies, sugars, and gel frosting as desired.

witches' broomsticks

supplies

12 7-inch pretzel rods, 3/8 inch thick
6 pieces fruit-flavored licorice twists
Cherry or apricot rolled fruit leather
Black or red licorice string

what to do

1 Cut pretzel to 6-inch rods with a serrated knife. Quarter licorice twists lengthwise and then cut into 2-inch pieces. Place about 10 pieces around the cut end of a pretzel rod. Using an 8×1-inch piece of fruit leather, tightly wrap around the end of pretzel, securing the fruit licorice to the pretzel and pressing fruit leather in place. Tie with a small piece of licorice string. Snip ends of fruit licorice with scissors to form broom fringe. Makes 12.

jack -o'- lantern treat totes

Crepe paper isn't just for decorating ceilings anymore! Cut small squares from the roll and decoupage the pieces over a balloon to create a pumpkin shell that's all ready to carve. Fill with shredded paper pieces and wrapped goodies for little ones to enjoy. The instructions are on page 53.

supplies

Newspapers
Small balloons
Disposable foam
 plate
Crafts knife
Scissors
Orange crepe
 paper
Decoupage
 medium
Paintbrush
Small foam ball,
 such as
 Styrofoam
Colored papers in
 yellow, black,
 and purple
Thick white
 crafts glue
Small paper
 punch
Eyelets and
 eyelet tool
Plastic-coated
 colored wires in
 purple, black,
 white, orange,
 yellow, and
 green
Ice pick or skewer

what to do

1 Cover your work surface with newspapers. Blow up a balloon to be about the size of a baseball. Secure the end.

2 Cut a small X in the center of the foam plate using a crafts knife. From the top of the plate, pull the knot of the balloon to the back of the plate. This will help hold the balloon while you work.

3 Use scissors to cut several squares from the crepe paper roll. Cover the bottom two-thirds of the balloon with a coat of decoupage medium. Add crepe paper squares over this area, using decoupage medium to stick the pieces to the balloon. Continue adding more crepe paper squares until at least two layers cover the entire two-thirds of the balloon. Paint a coat of decoupage medium over the crepe paper. Let it dry.

4 Pop the balloon and remove it. Place a foam ball inside the crepe paper cup. Use a crafts knife to cut the desired face in one side.

5 Cut a circle or oval from the desired color of paper to fit inside the crepe paper cup, underneath the cut features. Glue the paper in place and let the glue dry.

6 Punch a hole on each side of the face, approximately 1 inch from the top. Insert an eyelet in the hole and secure it using the eyelet tool as directed on the tool package.

7 Braid or twist wires together to make a handle. Insert the wire ends through the eyelet holes. To finish the wire ends, wrap them around an ice pick or skewer.

surprise sacks

Get ready for candy riches with these bags trimmed in felt, buttons, and stitches! Find bags like these in a gift wrap department, or glue jute handles to brown paper lunch bags as an alternative. The patterns and instructions are on pages 56–57.

55

SCAREDY CAT

CAT PATTERN

OH PUMPKIN PUMPKIN PUMPKIN

PUMPKIN PATTERN

surprise sacks continued

supplies

Tracing paper
Pencil
Scissors
**Felt sheets in
  black, orange,
  green, and white**
**Sewing threads in
  orange and black**
Sewing needle
**1 orange and
  4 blue beads**
Glue stick
**5x8-inch brown
  paper bags**
**Cotton
  embroidery
  floss in black,
  emerald green,
  and burnt orange**
**Assorted buttons
  in black, yellow,
  green, orange,
  and Halloween
  motifs**

what to do

1 Trace the
patterns,
opposite and *right,*
onto tracing paper
and cut out. Using
patterns, cut one
of each pumpkin
on orange felt,
three pumpkin
stems on green
felt, one cat on
black felt, and
two ghosts on
white felt. Cut
out shapes.

2 Stitch two blue
beads on each
ghost and one
orange bead to cat
for eyes. Glue the
felt shapes to
paper bags
using the
photo on
pages 54–55
for placement.

3 Use three
strands of
floss to stitch
straight stitches
around the
edges of the
felt shapes.
Stitch the
pumpkin with
emerald green
floss, the cat with
burnt orange floss,
and the ghosts
with emerald
green floss.

4 With a pencil,
lightly write
"OH PUMPKIN
PUMPKIN" on the
pumpkin bag,
"SCAREDY CAT"
on the cat bag, and
"CATCH ME" and
"BOO" on the
ghost bag. Draw
curly vines to the
center pumpkin
stem. Using three
strands of floss,
stitch straight
stitches to stitch
"OH PUMPKIN
PUMPKIN,"
"SCAREDY CAT,"
and vines with
emerald green
floss; "CATCH ME"
with black floss;
and "BOO" with
burnt orange floss.

5 Stitch the
buttons on the
bags as desired.

CATCH ME

BOO

**GHOST
PATTERN**

57

haunting
Scare them all night

decorations

masquerade ball wreath

Glittered wood masks add mysterious flair to this simple ring of grapevine. Cut the variety of mask shapes from plywood and drill holes at each side to attach them to the wreath. Wrap the entire ring with metallic star garland and this Halloween wreath gets the party off to an enchanting start.

supplies

Tracing paper
Pencil; scissors
¼-inch-thick
  plywood
Jigsaw
Drill and ⅛-inch
  bit
Wood glue
Medium
  sandpaper
Acrylic paint in
  light green,
  orange, purple,
  and yellow
Paintbrush
Glitter in blue
  and multicolors
Wire
18-inch grapevine
  wreath
Multicolored star
  garland

what to do

1 Trace the patterns, *pages 62–63,* onto tracing paper and cut out. Trace around the shapes on the sheet of plywood.

2 Cut out the mask shapes using a jigsaw. To cut out the eyes, first drill a hole in each eye area on the mask. Use the hole as a starting area to cut out each eye shape. Drill side holes where indicated. For the masks with the nose pieces, cut two nose pieces. On the long edge, cut at a 45-degree angle. Glue these edges together and let dry. Sand any rough edges until smooth. Glue to the face piece. Let dry.

3 Paint the masks with acrylic paint using the photograph, *opposite,* for ideas. Paint masks one at a time and, while the paint is wet, sprinkle the desired color of glitter onto the paint. Let the paint dry. Shake off any excess glitter.

4 Cut ten 4-inch-long pieces of wire. Thread one piece through each side hole in the masks. Twist the ends to secure. Use these wires to attach the masks to the wreath.

5 Wrap the wreath with star garland as desired.

continued on page 62

NOSE
PIECE
PATTERN
(CUT 2)

BLUE
MASK
PATTERN

GOLD
MASK
PATTERN

GREEN
MASK
PATTERN

PURPLE
MASK
PATTERN

NOSE
PIECE
PATTERN
(CUT 2)

RED MASK
PATTERN

63

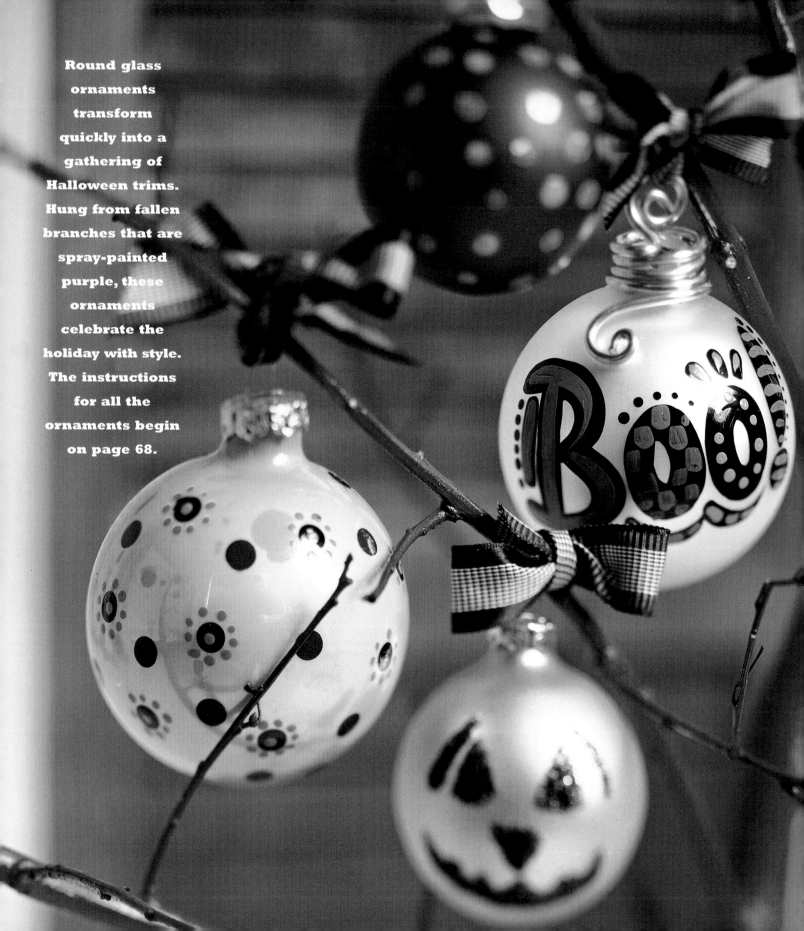

Round glass ornaments transform quickly into a gathering of Halloween trims. Hung from fallen branches that are spray-painted purple, these ornaments celebrate the holiday with style. The instructions for all the ornaments begin on page 68.

halloween tree trims

JACK-O'-LANTERN ORNAMENT

HALLOWEEN SWIRL ORNAMENT

65

**POLKA-DOT
ORNAMENTS**

**STARRY NIGHT
ORNAMENT**

**SPIDER-'N'-WEB
ORNAMENT**

**BOO-TO-YOU
ORNAMENT**

polka-dot ornaments

supplies

Round purple or
green ornament
Newspapers; string
Glass paints in
black, orange,
yellow, purple,
and green
Disposable foam
plate
Pencil with
round-tip eraser
Clear iridescent
glitter, if desired
Toothpick or
paintbrush
5 inches of lime
green sequins on
a string; thick
white crafts glue
⅛- to ¼-inch-wide
ribbon

what to do

1 Wash and dry
the ornament.
Avoid touching the
areas to be painted.

2 Cover the
work surface
with newspapers.
Tie a temporary
string hanger onto

3 Place desired
paint colors on
a plate. To make
large dots, dip the
eraser end of a
pencil into the
paint and dot onto
the ornament. If
desired, sprinkle
with glitter. To
make small dots,
use the end of a
toothpick or the
handle end of a
paintbrush. Let dry.

4 Glue sequin
string around
the ornament top.
Let the glue dry.
Use a 10-inch
piece of ribbon
to make the
permanent hanger.
Tie into a bow or
knot as desired.

jack-o'-lantern ornament

supplies

Round white or
orange glass
ornament
Pencil; newspapers
Thick white crafts

Glitter in black
or pink
⅛- to ¼-inch-wide
ribbon

what to do

1 Gently draw a
pumpkin face
on the ornament
using pencil. Press
lightly so as not to
break the ornament.

2 Cover work
surface with
newspapers. Draw
on facial features
using glue. While
wet, sprinkle on
glitter. Let dry.

3 Tie a ribbon
bow at the top.

starry night ornament

supplies

Round orange
glass ornament
Drinking glass
Gems in round and
star shapes in
clear and orange
Thick white
crafts glue
Black and gold
cording

what to do

1 Set the
ornament in
the glass while
working on
one side.

2 Glue gems to
the ornament
as desired. Let dry.
Turn the ornament
over. Glue gems to
the remaining side.
Let the glue dry.

3 Wrap and glue
cord around the
top. Let dry. Add a
cord hanger.

spider-'n'-web ornament

supplies

¼-inch-wide
rubber bands
Round orange
glass ornament
Newspapers
Black spray paint
5 inches of orange
sequins on a string
Spider ring
⅛-inch-wide satin
ribbon

BOO!

what to do

1 Place a rubber band around the center of the ornament. Place a second band over the topper and around the bottom (the bands will cross in the center). Place two rubber bands between those already on the ornament, making sure all intersect in the same place.

2 In a well-ventilated area, cover work surface with newspapers. Spray-paint a light coat over the ornament. Let dry. Remove the bands.

3 Glue the sequin string around the top. Let dry. Add a spider ring and ribbon hanger.

halloween swirl ornament

supplies

Round clear glass ornament with removable topper
Newspapers
Acrylic paints in black, yellow, and orange
Thick white crafts glue
2-inch piece of rhinestone trim
1-inch-wide metallic ribbon

what to do

1 Remove the topper from the ornament. Set the topper aside.

2 Cover work surface with newspapers. Put small amounts of black, orange, and yellow paints into the ornament. Rotate the ornament so the paints swirl together and the entire inside is covered with paint. Leave the topper off and let dry.

3 Place the topper on the ornament. Glue the rhinestone trim around the ornament top, trimming to fit. Let the glue dry. Thread the ribbon through the ornament top for a hanger.

boo-to-you ornament

supplies

Round white glass ornament
Glass paints in black, purple, green, yellow, and orange
Paintbrush
Needle-nose pliers
12-inch-long piece of lead-free solder
Clear silicone glue
Ribbon (optional)

what to do

1 Gently wash and dry the glass ornament. Avoid touching the areas on the ornament that will be painted.

2 Looking at the pattern, *above,* as a guide, paint the word "BOO" and the exclamation point in black. Let the paint dry.

3 Add the colored accents as shown, leaving a black border. Let the paint dry.

4 Use a needle-nose pliers to curl the ends of the solder. Form one end over the B on the ornament and carefully wrap the ornament top with the solder. Glue the solder in place. Let the glue dry. To hang, use the top solder loop or add a ribbon.

bewitching trims

Just minutes before you open the door to Halloween guests, make these striking candles and ornaments using wax stickers. Just peel and press and you're ready to entertain with creepy, clever trims throughout your very own haunted house.

creepy candles

supplies

Candle wax stickers in Halloween designs
Candles in a variety of shapes, sizes, and colors
Raffia, if desired

what to do

1 Decide the desired placement of the wax stickers.

2 Carefully peel off the wax shapes from the paper. Position them gently on the candles, pressing in place until the shapes adhere to the candles.

3 Tie a raffia bow around the candle bottom if desired. Remove the raffia when burning the candle.

terrifying trim

supplies

Candle wax stickers in bat or other desired designs
Round white glass ornament
$\frac{1}{4}$-inch-wide ribbon
Scissors

what to do

1 Carefully peel off the wax shapes from the paper. Position them gently on the ornament, pressing in place until the shapes adhere.

2 Add a ribbon hanger to the ornament top. Trim the ribbon ends.

holiday greetings wreath

Set a magical mood by making this quick and inexpensive wreath to welcome all the little folks on Beggars' Night. All it takes are white pony beads sprinkled between twists of colored chenille sticks to add Halloween sparkle to a grapevine wreath coated in glossy black paint.

supplies
- Newspapers
- 24-inch grapevine wreath
- Black, glossy spray paint
- Chenille stems in orange, silver, and black
- Round pencil
- Scissors
- White pony beads
- 1 yard of 2-inch-wide silver wired-edge ribbon

what to do

1 In a well-ventilated area, cover the work surface with newspapers. Lay the grapevine wreath on the newspapers and spray-paint one side of the wreath using black glossy paint. Let the paint dry. Turn the wreath over and spray-paint the back side. Let the paint dry.

2 Shape several orange and silver chenille stems into coils or S-shapes as shown in the photograph, *opposite*. Arrange the coils and S-shapes on the wreath and secure by wrapping one end of each chenille stem around a vine on the wreath.

3 To make each long spiral, wrap an orange chenille stem around a pencil. Remove the spiral from the pencil and tuck it into the wreath where desired, securing under the vines. Make six or seven spirals and attach them to the wreath.

4 Cut several 2-inch pieces from black chenille stems. Thread a white pony bead on each chenille stem piece. Twist each beaded chenille stem piece around the vine wreath. Continue adding beads between the chenille shapes until the desired look is achieved.

5 Decide where the bow will be placed on the wreath. Slip the piece of ribbon under some of the vines where the bow is desired. Tie the ribbon into a bow. Trim the ribbon ends as needed.

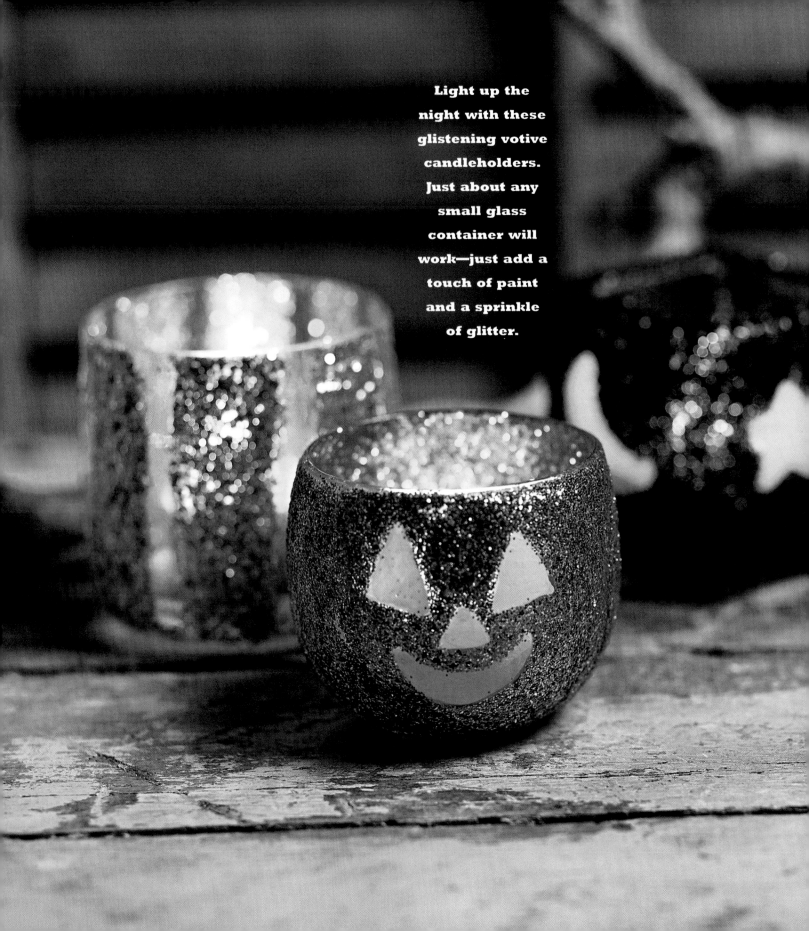

Light up the night with these glistening votive candleholders. Just about any small glass container will work—just add a touch of paint and a sprinkle of glitter.

very scary candleholders

supplies

Tracing paper
Pencil
Scissors
Votive candleholders or any small glass containers
Masking tape
Yellow glass paint
Paintbrush
Decoupage medium
Glitter in orange, green, and black

what to do

1 Trace the moon, star, and jack-o'-lantern patterns at *right* onto tracing paper. Cut out each pattern or grouping about ½ inch from the edge of the design.

2 Wash and dry the glass container. Avoid touching the areas to be painted. Tape the desired pattern inside the glass container. Using the pattern as a guide, paint inside the shapes using glass paint. Let the paint dry. Bake the glass item in the oven if directed by paint instructions.

3 Coat the outer surface of the glass container with decoupage medium, except the painted areas and the bottom of the container. Sprinkle glitter over the wet decoupage medium until well covered. Let it dry.

4 Brush off the excess glitter and put a light final coat of decoupage medium over the glittered areas only. Do not submerse the votive holder in water.

MOON
PATTERN

STAR
PATTERN

JACK-O'-LANTERN
PATTERN

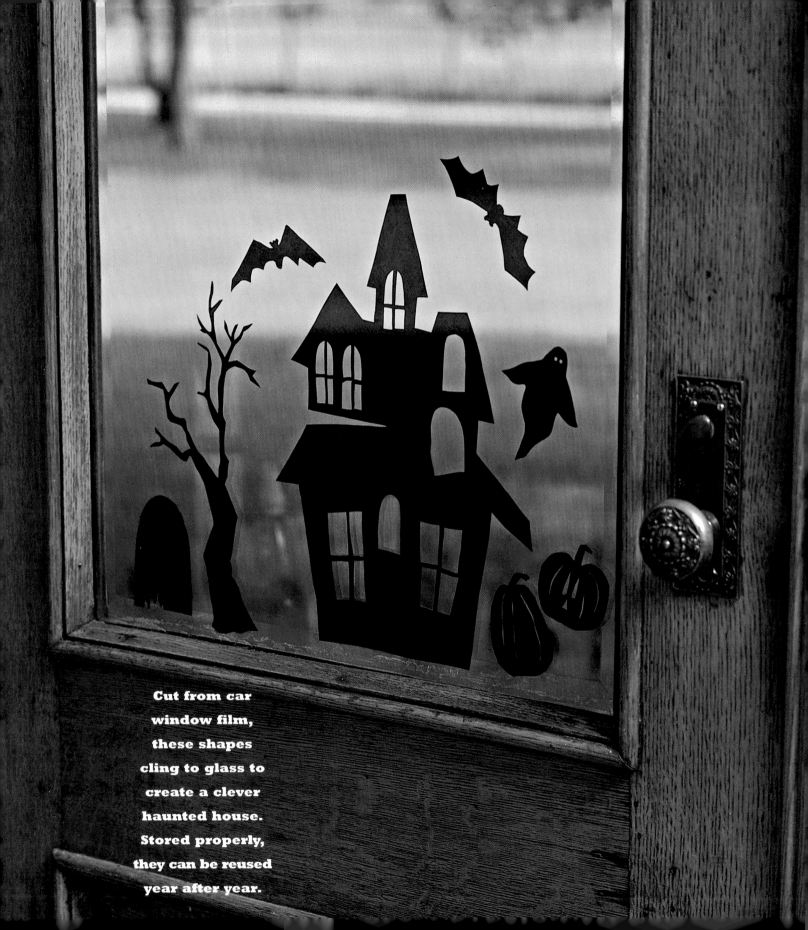

Cut from car
window film,
these shapes
cling to glass to
create a clever
haunted house.
Stored properly,
they can be reused
year after year.

spooky window scene

supplies

Static cling black window film for car glass
Permanent black marking pen
Scissors
Cutting board
Crafts knife

what to do

1 Using a marking pen, trace the patterns, *below* and *pages 78–79,* onto the film. Cut out the shapes with scissors.

2 On a cutting board, use a crafts knife to cut out the inside details. If it is difficult to see the drawn lines, slip a piece of white paper between the cutting board and the film before cutting.

3 Apply the film pieces to a window by gently rubbing each film piece to remove the bubbles. If necessary, wipe the window with a damp rag to help the film stick.

4 To remove the cutouts, gently peel the film off the window. To store the pieces, keep them separate with sheets of paper between them and store flat.

GHOST PATTERN

JACK-O'-LANTERN PATTERN

PUMPKIN PATTERN

BAT PATTERNS

TOMBSTONE PATTERN

TREE PATTERN

1 square = 1 inch

1 square = 1 inch

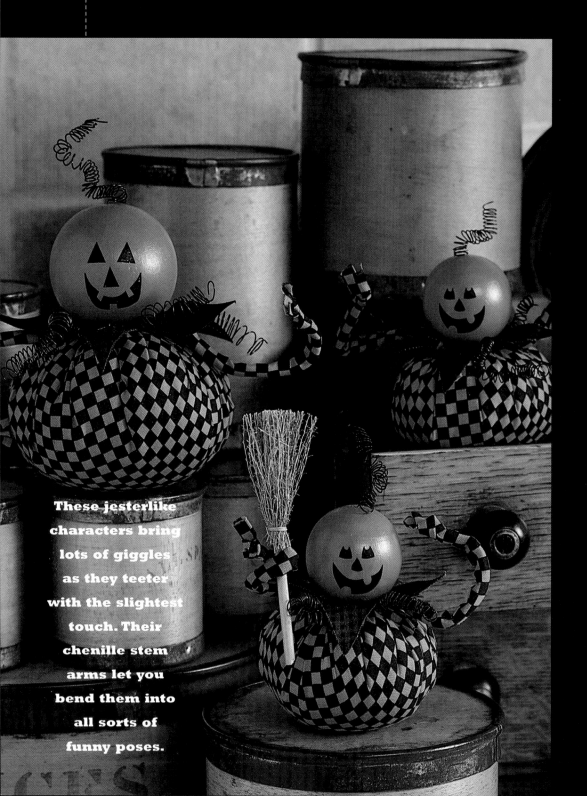

These jesterlike characters bring lots of giggles as they teeter with the slightest touch. Their chenille stem arms let you bend them into all sorts of funny poses.

supplies

Pencil
Tracing paper
Scissors; compass
Two 7-inch squares of green-and-black plaid fabric
7x7-inch piece of paper-backed fusible web
$\frac{1}{4}$ yard of orange-and-black checked fabric
2-inch-diameter wood knob with flat side
Two $1\frac{1}{2}$-inch-diameter wood knobs, each with one flat side
Acrylic paints in orange and black
Paintbrush
Heavy black thread
Sewing needle
Polyester fiberfill
Hot-glue gun and hot-glue sticks
3 chenille stems
Liquid seam sealant
$3\frac{1}{2}$-inch-long straw broom
5 yards of 30-gauge florist's wire
T-pin

FACE AND LEAF PATTERNS

what to do

1 Trace the leaf patterns, *right,* onto tracing paper. Cut out. For small body pattern, use a compass and draw a circle 6¾ inches across onto tracing paper and cut out. For the large body pattern, draw a circle 8¼ inches across onto tracing paper and cut out.

2 To make the leaves, fuse the green-and-black fabric squares together using fusible web.

3 From orange-and-black fabric, use patterns to cut one large body, two small bodies, and one 1⅛×12½-inch strip, and two 1⅛×10½-inch strips for arms. From double-sided fabric, cut 5 large and 10 small leaves.

4 Paint the knobs orange. Let dry.

With flat sides down, paint faces on the knobs, using the patterns, *right,* as a guide. Let dry.

5 For each body, use a double strand of heavy thread to sew a running stitch ¼ inch from edge of fabric. Stuff with fiberfill. Pull threads and knot.

6 For leaves, make a tuck in rounded end, glue to neck. Hot-glue heads to bodies.

7 For arms, cut chenille stems into one 10-inch-long and two 8-inch-long pieces. Apply liquid seam sealant to short ends of orange-and-black fabric strips. Let dry. Press under ¼ inch on one long side of each fabric strip. Tie a knot ½ inch from one end of each fabric strip. Push one end of

long chenille stem up against the knot of the long fabric strip. Wrap fabric around chenille stem with pressed edge covering raw edge. Slip-stitch closed. Tie a knot in the remaining end of the fabric strip ½ inch from the end, working the knot down against the end of the chenille stem. Repeat, using the shorter fabric strips and chenille stems.

8 To attach arms, center the longer arm behind the head and underneath the leaves of the larger body. Shape arms to fit curve of head. Glue in place. Attach the arms to the small figures in the same manner.

9 Glue the broom to a character as desired. Let dry.

10 For tendrils, cut florist's wire into twelve 15-inch-long pieces. To curl the wire, wrap each piece around a pencil. Slip off pencil. Apply glue to one end of a tendril and slip it between the leaves, pressing the end into the body. Glue three tendrils around each head. Use a T-pin to make a small hole about ¼ inch deep in the top of each head. Glue one tendril to the top of each head.

Crank up the "Monster Mash" and give this gal a tap! With a funnel used for a body, this happy-go-lucky witch will bob to the beat and have you smiling in no time.

supplies

- Two 6x$\frac{1}{2}$-inch wood dowels
- Acrylic paints in black, orange, and purple
- Paintbrush
- 2 wood hearts approximately 2x1x$\frac{3}{16}$ inches
- 1x$\frac{1}{2}$-inch wood dowel
- Hot-glue gun and hot-glue sticks
- Small wood base
- Paint pens in black, green, orange, and glitter gold
- Scissors
- 4-inch plastic funnel
- Black spray paint
- Tracing paper
- Pencil
- Sheet of white card stock
- Permanent marking pens in black, and green
- Red colored pencil
- Thick white crafts glue
- Scrap of yellow paper

HAT STAR
PATTERN

COAT STAR
PATTERN

FRONT/BACK
HEAD AND HAT
PATTERN

ARM
PATTERN

what to do

1 For legs, paint the 6-inch-long dowels with orange and purple stripes. Paint the hearts black for shoes. Let the paint dry.

2 Hot-glue the bottom of each dowel to the center back of one heart. The pointed portion of the heart becomes the toe of the shoe. Hot-glue the legs together by gluing the 1×½-inch wood dowel spacer between the top of each leg. Hot-glue the shoes to the wood base. Use glitter gold to squeeze three gold buttons down the center of each shoe.

3 With heavy-duty scissors, cut the handle from the funnel if necessary. Spray-paint the funnel black and set aside

4 Trace the patterns, *right,* onto tracing paper and cut out. Cut the front (with chin) and the back (without chin) head pieces from card stock. Color the hat black using marking pen. Use green to color the hair as shown, *right,* for front. For back, color entire head area with green. Draw in face details using black. Color the mouth and cheeks with red pencil. Outline the hat with black paint pen. Add a gold hat band. Add strokes of green and gold to hair.

5 Cut a length of card stock to go around the neck of the funnel. Color it with black. Glue strip around neck

head front to one side of tube and head back to the opposite side.

6 Cut arms from card stock. Color the sleeves black and add orange paint-pen stripes to each cuff area. Outline the stripes with black paint pen. Let the

7 Use crafts glue to glue the arms to the sides of the body. Add buttons down the front of the body using glitter gold paint pen.

8 Cut stars from yellow paper and glue the large one to coat and the small one to the tip

Serve up delicious concoctions on a wood tray touting an inlay of small broken tiles in the shape of a pumpkin.

mosaic pumpkin tray

supplies

Tracing paper
Pencil
Scissors
15x11x3-inch wood serving tray
Safety glasses
Crafting mosaic tiles: 2 bags of orange, 2 bags of green, and 3 bags of white
Tile-cutting nipper
Hammer
Towels
Crafts stick
Mosaics adhesive
Mosaics white sanded tile grout
Spatula
Rag or sponge
Green acrylic paint
Paintbrush
Satin varnish

what to do

1 Enlarge and trace the pumpkin pattern, *below,* onto tracing paper. Cut out the pattern.

2 Place the pattern in the center of the tray and trace around the shape.

3 Put on safety glasses before breaking tiles. Cut tiles into various shapes with a cutting nipper and hammer. To break tiles with a hammer, put them on a towel with the colored surface down. Cover with a towel and strike with a hammer.

4 Use a crafts stick to spread adhesive on small sections of the wood at a time. Glue orange tile chips inside the pumpkin outline. Glue green tile chips for the stem and to form a border around the edge of the tray bottom. Fill in the remaining spaces with white tile chips.

5 Mix the grout according to the manufacturer's instructions. Spread grout on the top of the tiles with a spatula and your fingers, pressing the grout in spaces between tiles. Wipe grout off the top of tiles with a damp sponge or rag. Let it set up.

6 Paint the tray green. Let it dry. Apply a coat of varnish over the paint. Let it dry.

PUMPKIN PATTERN

1 square = 1 inch

85

jack-o'-lantern centerpiece

Any type of jack-o'-lantern, carved or made of foam, will take on a bewitching personality when topped with this star-struck hat. The purchased hat is embellished with purple and orange glitter. Placed on a handful of shredded mylar, this clever creation makes a stunning centerpiece. For extra shrieks, place a plastic lizard or frog on the brim.

supplies
Tracing paper
Pencil
Scissors
White pencil
Witch hat
Lime green paint pen
Thick white crafts glue
Paintbrush
Glitter in purple and orange
Foam or carved jack-o'-lantern
Shredded mylar
Plastic lizard or frog

what to do

1 Trace star patterns, *right*, and cut out. Use white pencil to trace around star shapes on witch hat.

2 Use a lime green paint pen to draw over star shapes. Let the paint pen dry.

3 Paint a thin coat of crafts glue inside each drawn star shape. While the glue is wet, sprinkle it with the desired color of glitter. Let it dry and shake off the excess glitter.

4 Place jack-o'-lantern on a handful of shredded mylar. Arrange the hat on top of the jack-o'-lantern, adding a plastic lizard or frog to the brim.

SMALL STAR PATTERN

LARGE STAR PATTERN

87

ghoulish garlands

Whatever the theme of your Halloween decorating, you'll find a garland that fits right into the plan. From funky witch hats to gem-embellished masks and dancing candy corn with pony bead spacers—these festive trims will add holiday pizzazz to doors, mantels, windows, banisters, and more!

supplies

Tracing paper
Pencil
Scissors
White pencil
Crafting foam in orange, yellow, white, purple, green, and black
Round and star-shape paper punches
Pinking shears
Thick white crafts glue
Gems
Permanent silver marking pen
Plastic-coated colored wires
Chenille stems
Curling ribbon
Pony beads
Ice pick

what to do

1 Trace the desired garland patterns from *pages 90–91* onto tracing paper. Cut out shapes.

2 Trace around patterns as many times as desired on crafting foam. If pencil lines do not show up, use a white pencil. Cut out shapes.

3 To make tiny circle or star shapes, punch out with a paper punch. To make zigzag stripes, cut with a pinking shears.

4 Layer and glue pieces together, using the patterns as a guide. Let the glue dry.

5 Embellish the foam pieces by adding gems, small snippets of foam, or by drawing in details with silver marking pen.

6 To connect the garland pieces, use the photographs, *opposite* and *above,* for ideas. Use a paper punch to add holes if needed. Thread wire, chenille stems, or curling ribbon through the holes, adding beads if desired. To form wire into a spiral shape, wrap it around an ice pick before connecting it to foam shapes.

continued on page 90

ROUND AND SQUARE SPIRAL
PATTERNS

CANDY CORN
PATTERN

MASK
PATTERN

BOO!

BOO LETTERING PATTERN

SQUATTY WITCH HAT
PATTERN

TALL WITCH HAT
PATTERN

91

hallow's eve wind sock

When the chilly October winds blow, let this colorful trim catch each gust. The Halloween wind sock is stitched using several colors of yarn and simple stitches that work quickly over 7-count plastic canvas. The nylon streamers are edged with sequins on a string that sparkles even when the moon is shining.

supplies

Red Heart Super Saver worsted weight yarn in kiwi (651), bright yellow (324), black (312), lavender (358), white (311), and vibrant orange (354)
No. 13 tapestry needle
7-count plastic canvas, cut 85 holes × 35 holes
Cotton embroidery floss in black and white
Scissors
Hot-glue gun and hot-glue sticks
1 yard of black nylon fabric
Cutting mat
Rotary cutter
Ruler
Approximately 20 yards of orange and black sequins on a string

what to do

1 Following the chart on *page 95,* stitch the design on plastic canvas using the continental stitch. Do not stitch the first four columns of the left edge of the design. Start in the fifth hole at the top left, beginning with the fifth stitch. Stitch all French knots using four strands of floss.

2 After stitching is completed, except for the four left columns, fold the plastic canvas to form a tube. Overlap the four columns of holes on each end and finish stitching the design, going through both layers of canvas to join the ends.

continued on page 94

3 Overcast the top and the bottom edges using black yarn.

4 Cut two 30-inch lengths from orange, kiwi, and black yarns. Tie the yarns together on one end and divide the yarns into the two yarns of each color. Braid together for 17 inches. Tie the yarns together at the end of the braid and trim any excess yarn. Glue one end inside the top of the plastic canvas tube and glue the other end on the opposite side to form a hanger.

5 Spread nylon fabric on the cutting mat. Use a rotary cutter to cut the fabric into 10 lengthwise strips that are 2 inches wide. Stop cutting 1 inch from the top edge. Apply glue along the long sides and press sequins along edge. Let the glue dry. Apply glue along the bottom inside edge of the plastic canvas tube ½ inch from the bottom. Glue the top edge of the nylon streamers to the tube.

NYLON FABRIC CUTTING DIAGRAM

CONTINENTAL STITCH

FRENCH KNOT

**HALLOW'S EVE WIND SOCK
CHART AND COLOR KEY**

Coats Red Heart (Super Saver)
- 311 White
- 312 Black
- 324 Bright yellow
- 354 Vibrant orange
- 358 Lavender
- 651 Kiwi

FRENCH KNOT
- ○ 000 DMC White
- ● 310 DMC Black

clever

Get in the spirit

costumes

crazy caterpillar

For a group of young friends, this prizewinning costume gives getting together a whole new meaning. Created from a length of lime green felt, the caterpillar's coat is decorated with bright, irregular spots.

supplies
Paper; pencil
Tape measure
2½ yards of
  72-inch-wide
  lime green felt
Scissors
Large yellow
  buttons
Sewing needle
Thread
½ yard of
  72-inch-wide
  black felt
Thick white crafts
  glue
½ yard of
  72-inch-wide
  each of pink and
  yellow felt
Pinking shears
Tracing paper
Headband
Metallic chenille
  stems
Two large pink
  pom-poms
Purchased black
  pants and
  sweatshirts, white
  tennis shoes, and
  green baseball
  hats and gloves

what to do
1 Use paper to make an oval arm opening pattern, 12 inches high and 6 inches wide. Make a circular 6-inch-diameter neck opening pattern.

2 Fold green felt in half lengthwise as shown on the diagram, *page 100.* Use the patterns to start marking the neck holes 4 inches from the front end at the fold. Leaving 18 inches between neck holes, mark the remaining three neck holes. Cut out the four neck holes.

3 For each arm opening, trace around the pattern 4 inches from the neck opening. Cut out the eight arm holes.

4 Cut scallops across bottom, from centers of armholes as shown in the diagram on *page 100.* Cut front into a vest shape and angle the back to create the look of a tail.

5 Overlap front vest pieces and secure by sewing on large buttons. Stitch back seam.

6 Cut eight 4x24-inch strips from black felt. Glue strips below armholes, trimming to match the bottom scallop.

7 Cut six 8½-inch circles from pink felt using pinking shears. Enlarge and trace the pattern, *page 101.* Use the pattern to cut six shapes from yellow felt using scissors. Glue the cutouts as shown, *left.*

8 For antennae, wrap chenille stems around a headband. Glue pom-poms to ends of two stems and wrap around sides of headband. Place over the hat of the leader.

continued on page 100

CATERPILLAR DIAGRAM

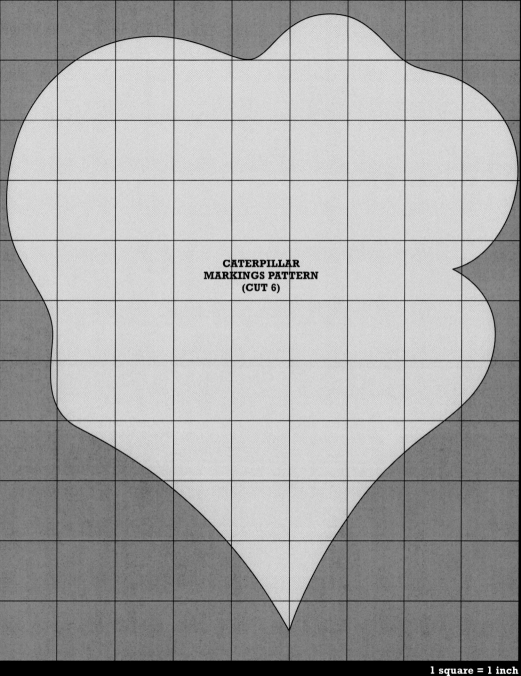

**CATERPILLAR
MARKINGS PATTERN
(CUT 6)**

1 square = 1 inch

cleopatra

Look like the queen of Egypt herself with this golden costume embellished with gems of all colors. An elegant gold doily, dripping with beads, adds the crowning touch.

supplies

Scissors
3 yards of 45-inch-wide metallic knit fabric with sequins
Thread
Sewing needle
Two 9-inch pieces of ½-inch-wide elastic
1 yard of 45-inch-wide quilted lamé
4 yards of ½-inch-wide sequin trim
Fabric glue
Assorted acrylic gems; gem glue
1 yard of ¼-inch-wide grosgrain ribbon
1¼ yards of 4-inch-wide sequined elastic
4 yards of gold beads on a string
8-inch-diameter gold crocheted doily
1 yard of 2-inch-wide sequined elastic
Sandals
Glitter face paint

what to do

1 Cut an 8-inch neck opening in the center of the metallic knit fabric. Fold the fabric piece in half, right sides together, with the short ends meeting. Sew the side seams, allowing 10-inch arm openings and 10-inch bottom slits on both sides. Turn.

2 Along each shoulder, stretch and stitch a 9-inch piece of elastic to the inside of the garment.

3 For collar, use the diagram on *page 104* as a guide to cut a 17-inch-diameter circle from lamé. Cut a 5-inch-diameter circle in the center for neck opening. Cut center back open. Topstitch a tiny hem around all edges. Glue the sequin trim to collar edge. Add gems to the collar where desired. Stitch ribbons to each corner of the center back opening for ties.

4 For belt apron, enlarge and trace pattern from *page 105*. Cut the shape from gold lamé. Glue the trim and gems to the belt apron as shown in the photographs, *above*. Cut the 4-inch-wide sequined elastic to a comfortable waist measurement plus seams. Stitch the apron to the center front of 4-inch-wide sequined elastic belt. Stitch center back seam of belt.

5 For headpiece, cut the beaded string into ten equal pieces. Sew five to each side of doily as shown, *opposite*. Glue on gems as desired. Let the glue dry.

6 To make upper arm bands, cut 2-inch-wide sequined elastic two inches larger than upper arm measurement. Sew a 1-inch seam, tacking ends to back of elastic.

continued on page 104

CLEOPATRA
COLLAR
DIAGRAM

17"

5"

look-at-me costumes

A smart alternative to a mask, this little mouse has a painted face made from supplies around the house. Add easy-sew ears to a headband to complete the look.

Let a child's imagination soar with a lofty costume created from a recycled box.

Or, create a caveman with fake fur and spray paint.

squeaky the mouse

supplies

For costume:
Tracing paper
Pencil
Scissors
⅓ yard gray felt
9x12-inch piece of pink felt
Thick white crafts glue
Chenille stem
Stapler
1 yard pink baby rickrack
White plastic headband
Hot-glue gun and hot-glue sticks
Small, natural sponge

White acrylic paint
Gray hooded sweat suit

For face paints:
1 teaspoon cornstarch
½ teaspoon cold cream
Mixing bowl
½ teaspoon water
Muffin tin
Food coloring
Small paintbrush or cotton swab

what to do

1 Enlarge and trace the mouse ear patterns, *right,* and cut out. Cut two outer ears from gray felt. Cut two inner ears from pink felt.

2 Glue an inner ear atop each outer ear, sandwiching half of a chenille stem between. Tuck each ear, securing with a staple along the bottom edge. Glue rickrack around the outer edge of each inner ear.

3 Cut a strip of gray felt the length and width of the headband. Glue the strip around the top of the headband, trimming as necessary to match the edges. Bend the bottom 1 inch of each ear forward at a 90-degree angle. Hot-glue the bent portion of each ear to the underside of the headband.

4 Dip a moist sponge into a puddle of white paint; sponge-paint the gray on the ears and headband. Let the paint dry.

5 For face paint, stir together the cornstarch and cold cream in a mixing bowl until it is well blended. Add water and stir.

6 Decide how many colors of paint you want. Put a dab of the cold cream mixture into a muffin tin for each color. Add food coloring, one drop at a time, until the desired colors are achieved. Mix well.

7 Using the photograph, *opposite,* for inspiration, paint the cheeks and nose using a paintbrush or cotton swab. Add whiskers and other details as desired.

flying high airplane

supplies

Cardboard box appropriate for the size of the child
Duct tape
Utility knife
Tracing paper
Pencil
Extra flat pieces of cardboard
Hot-glue gun and hot-glue sticks
Plastic margarine tub
Newspapers
Spray paint in desired color
4x4x1-inch piece of wood
Drill and drill bit
Bolt slightly longer than margarine tub depth and a nut
Colored electrical tape
Two 30-inch-long pieces of 1½-inch fabric strapping

continued on page 108

MOUSE INNER EAR (CUT 2)   TUCK

MOUSE OUTER EAR (CUT 2)

CENTER SEAM   TUCK

SQUEAKY THE MOUSE PATTERNS

1 square = 2 inches

what to do

1 Fold flaps from the box bottom to the inside and tape in place. Fold the two side flaps from the top to the inside and tape in place. Using a utility knife, trim semicircles from the two remaining flaps to allow a child to stand in the box.

2 Enlarge and trace the plane patterns, *opposite*. Cut the shapes from cardboard.

3 Use hot-glue to attach the tail top to the center of the tail. Glue the two tail supports perpendicular to the underneath side of the tail, each about 2 inches from the center. Glue two supports to the underside of each wing, aligning with the outside edge as shown in the photo on *page 106*. With straight sides aligned, glue the propellers to the propeller center. Glue the propeller unit to the bottom of the margarine tub. Let all glue set.

4 In a well-ventilated area, cover your work surface with newspapers. Spray-paint all sides of the box and cardboard pieces. Let the paint dry.

5 Assemble the airplane using hot-glue and according to the photograph. To add the propeller, back it with the wood square inside the box. Drill a hole through the box and wood piece. Drill a hole in the center of the propeller. Secure in place with a nut and bolt.

6 Add stripes to the airplane as desired using electrical tape.

7 Cut two 1½-inch-long slits in each untaped box flap for shoulder straps. Insert the ends of the strapping through the slits. Adjust to fit child and knot the ends of the strapping.

tough-guy caveman

supplies

Spray paint in black, gray, and brown
⅞ yard of 60-inch-wide gray fake fur
Scissors; gray sewing thread
Sewing needle
Three 1-yard-long strips of brown leather
Vinyl dog bone
Fat baseball bat
Newspaper
Masking tape
Sandals

what to do

1 Spray-paint fake fur with stripes of gray and black as desired. Let the paint dry.

2 Cut a straight tunic front/back from painted fur. Cut a diamond shape in the center for the neck. Stitch side seams from bottom edge, leaving 10 inches open for each arm. Cut jagged points into the bottom.

3 For necklace, tie the center of one leather strip around one end of the bone. Knot ends.

4 For arm bands, tie leather strips in crisscross fashion around the upper arms. Tie the ends.

5 For club, pad bat with crumpled newspapers. Secure in place with masking tape. Wrap the entire bat with tape, covering the papers. Spray the club with gray and brown paint.

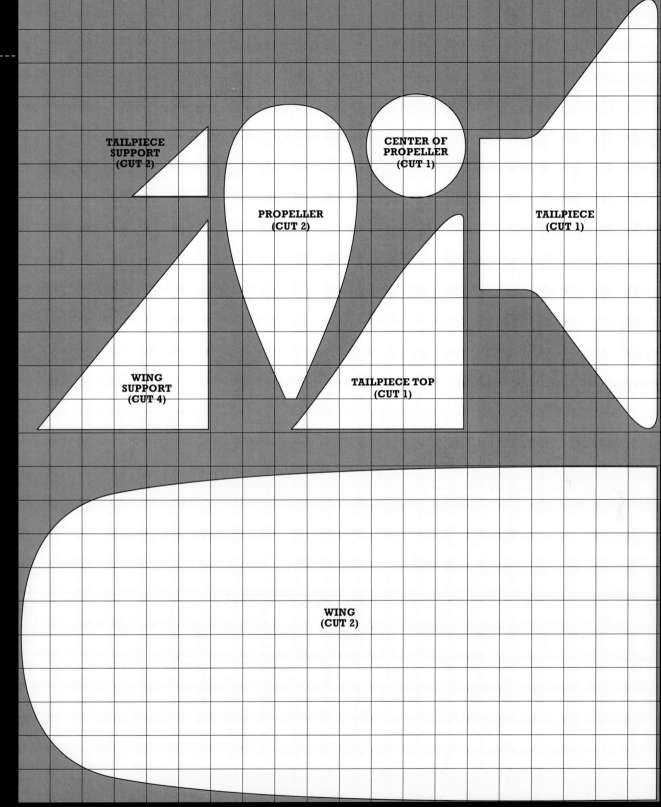

TAILPIECE
SUPPORT
(CUT 2)

CENTER OF
PROPELLER
(CUT 1)

PROPELLER
(CUT 2)

TAILPIECE
(CUT 1)

WING
SUPPORT
(CUT 4)

TAILPIECE TOP
(CUT 1)

WING
(CUT 2)

FLYING HIGH AIRPLANE PATTERNS

1 square = 1 inch

lu-lu the ladybug

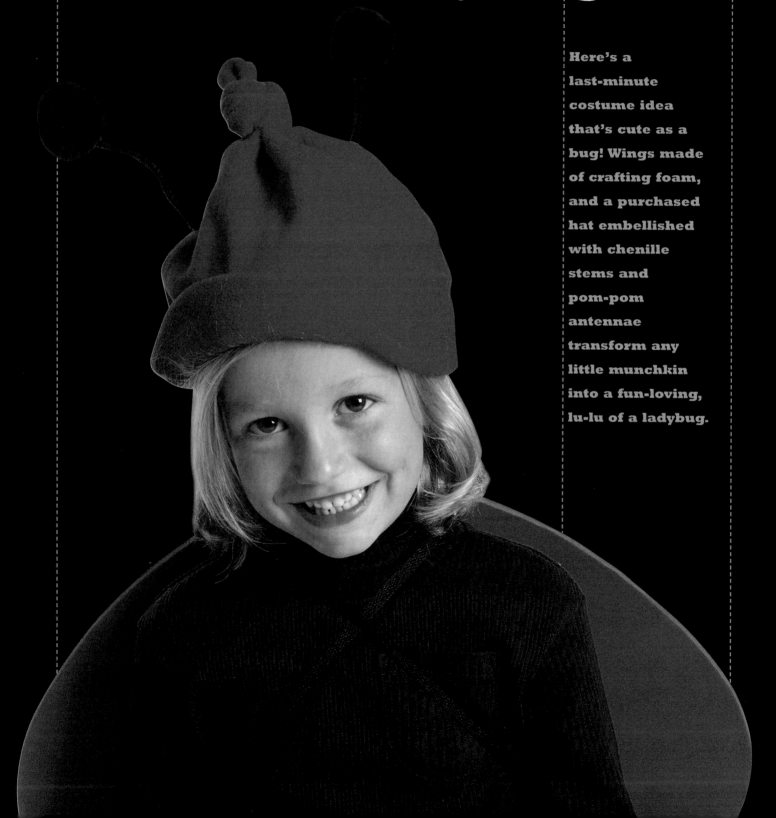

Here's a last-minute costume idea that's cute as a bug! Wings made of crafting foam, and a purchased hat embellished with chenille stems and pom-pom antennae transform any little munchkin into a fun-loving, lu-lu of a ladybug.

supplies
Pencil
Tracing paper
Scissors
¼-inch-thick red crafting foam
Thin black crafting foam
Hot-glue gun and hot-glue sticks
Paper punch
4 eyelets and eyelet punch
Pair of black 42-inch-long shoelaces
Purchased red hat and black gloves

Black chenille stem
Two large, black pom-poms

what to do

1 Enlarge and trace the wing pattern, *page 113,* onto tracing paper. Cut out. Trace the dot pattern and cut out. Cut two wings from red foam and six dots from the black foam.

2 Using the diagram, *page 112,* glue the short flat edges of the wings together. Glue three dots on each wing. Let the glue dry.

3 Use a paper punch to make two holes at the top of each wing. For reinforcement, add an eyelet to each.

4 Tie the shoelaces together at one end. Place the knot by the seam on the wrong side of the wings. Thread the laces through the holes in each wing.

5 For hat, poke a chenille stem through the top of the hat. Glue a pom-pom on each end. Let dry.

continued on page 112

111

LADYBUG
PLACEMENT
DIAGRAM

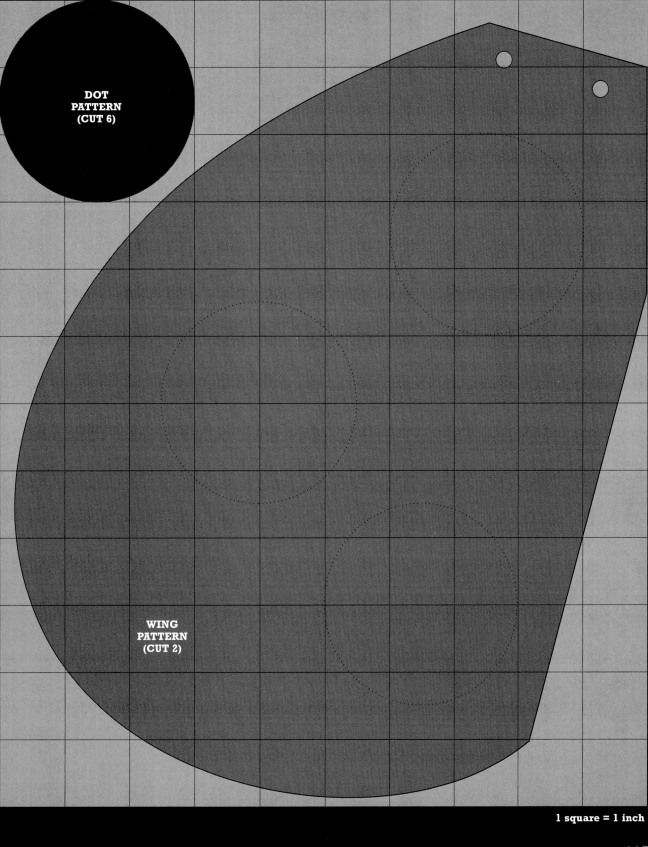

DOT
PATTERN
(CUT 6)

WING
PATTERN
(CUT 2)

1 square = 1 inch

A great Halloween costume no matter your age, this scarecrow seems to attract the birds rather than scare them away. Burlap patches and bits of raffia make this guy look like the real thing.

stanley scarecrow

supplies

Ruler; pencil
Fusible web paper
Scissors
Burlap in red,
  yellow, and blue
Bib overalls
Needle and thread
Straw hat
Raffia
Fine wire
Small and large
  artificial crows
Plaid shirt
3 bandanna
  handkerchiefs
Face paints in
  black and red
Eyeliner
Corncob pipe

what to do

1 To make patches, trace a 4-inch square onto web paper. Cut out and fuse to burlap. Cut burlap shapes 1 inch bigger on all sides. Fringe the outer edges. Arrange the patches on the overalls and fuse in place. Accent with running stitches if desired.

2 Trim hat with jagged cuts at the outer edge. Wire a band of raffia around the brim. Wire a small crow to the brim of the hat.

3 Hand-stitch raffia to the inside of the shirt cuffs and pant leg openings. Tuck bandannas into the bib pocket, shoulder strap, and back pocket. Wire the large crow to the top of an overall strap or around an arm.

4 Add face details such as red cheeks, eyebrows, and stitch marks using eyeliner and face paints. Tuck a corncob pipe in the bib pocket.

Step 1

Step 2

RUNNING STITCH

frankie the monster

You'll be doing the monster mash in style with this silly mask made from shiny vinyl place mats. Throw on a flea market jacket and you're ready for loads of Halloween fun.

supplies
Pencil
Tracing paper
Scissors
Vinyl place mats
  or crafting foam
  in lavender and
  lime green
Crafts knife
Thick white
  crafts glue
Paper punch
Pair of shoelaces

what to do

1 Enlarge the face and hair patterns, *right.* Trace all patterns onto tracing paper and cut out. Cut the face from green vinyl material and the rest of the pattern pieces from lavender. Use a crafts knife to cut out the eyeholes, mouth, and nose. Use scissors to cut a 1-inch-high T for neck bolt. Cut a ½-inch-long slit to hold the neck bolt.

MONSTER MASK PATTERNS

1 square = 1 inch

2 Overlap and glue the hair to the top of the head. Glue all of the face pieces in place, using the pattern as a guide. Let dry.

3 In line with eyeholes, use a paper punch to make a hole 1 inch from each mask edge. Tie a shoelace through each hole. Tie the shoelaces behind head to secure in place.

117

clarise the clown

Get ready to put on a happy face with this cheerful clown costume. Bright fabrics and rickrack turn an ordinary sweat suit into circuslike attire.

supplies

Pencil
Fusible web paper
Assorted bright
    solids and
    polka-dot fabric
Scissors
Blue sweat suit
Thread
Needle
4x72-inch piece
    of bright fabric
5x72-inch piece
    of coordinating
    bright fabric
2 yards each of
    jumbo rickrack
    in two colors

1 yard of ³⁄₈-inch-
    wide grosgrain
    ribbon
Purchased wig
Hairbands for cuffs
Face paints

what to do

1 Draw 4- and
5-inch-diameter
circles onto web
paper. Fuse to
bright fabrics.

Cut out the fabric
pieces and fuse to
the sweatshirt and
the sweatpants.
2 To make the
collar, stitch a
narrow hem on two
short ends and one
long side of each
bright fabric
rectangle. Topstitch
rickrack to each of
the long hemmed

edges. Layer the
narrow strip on top
of the wide strip
with the right sides
facing up. Stitch
the raw edges
together using a
¹⁄₄-inch seam
allowance. Press
the seam open.
3 Gather along
the seam to
about 18 inches.
Stitch the gathered
edge onto the
ribbon. Tie the
collar around
the neck.

all abuzz suits

Your little one will create quite a stir wearing these bold stripes. The tabard pattern could be easily enlarged for a matching adult version.

If you have only minutes to spare, make the cute frog getup, opposite. Just add the eyes and neck detail to a sweat suit and you're ready to go!

beatrice bee

supplies

Tracing paper
Pencil; scissors
24x48-inch piece of heavy sew-in interfacing
3 yards of 72-inch-wide black felt
¼ yard of 72-inch-wide yellow felt
Spray adhesive
Thick white crafts glue
6 yards of yellow medium rickrack
3 black loopy chenille stems
Black headband
Two 2-inch yellow pom-poms
Yellow gloves

what to do

1 Enlarge and trace patterns, *right*. Cut two tabards from interfacing and four from black felt. Cut two stingers from yellow felt.

2 Layer the interfacing tabards between felt tabards, using spray adhesive to temporarily secure layers. Machine-zigzag around neck and outer edges.

3 Cut six 3×22-inch yellow felt strips. Glue strips to tabard as indicated on pattern. Trim ends to match tabard. Glue yellow rickrack around neck and outer edges. Stitch an 18-inch-long piece of yellow rickrack to each side at the Xs to make ties.

4 Glue stinger points together, sandwiching one end of a chenille stem between. Stitch remaining end of chenille stem to dot on tabard back.

5 For antennae, twist one end of each remaining chenille stem around tip of headband. Glue a pom-pom to each tip. Let dry.

ready-to-leap frog

supplies

Scissors; ruler
¼ yard green felt
Fabric glue
Green hooded sweat suit, gloves, and swim fins
2 Ping-Pong balls
Permanent black marking pen

what to do

1 Cut nine 6-inch-long triangles from green felt. With narrow points down, glue around sweatshirt below hood. Let dry.

2 Cut two 4×7-inch pieces from felt. Align the center of one long edge with the center of a Ping-Pong ball. Shape and glue felt to ball at top and sides. Let dry.

3 Draw a dime-size dot in the middle of each Ping-Pong ball. Draw a slanted 1-inch-long line through each dot.

4 Glue the eyes to top of the hood. Let dry.

YELLOW (CUT 2)

BUMBLEBEE TABARD (CUT 2)

YELLOW (CUT 2)

FOLD

YELLOW (CUT 2)

STINGER (CUT 2)

BEATRICE BEE PATTERNS   1 square = 2 inches

chilling

Rattle those bones

parties

scare-me-silly party

From the moment they receive their imaginative invitations, party guests will know they're in for an unforgettable night of chills and little unexpected surprises. You can make the invites, right, using only a few supplies from around the house. And when it's time to quench the thirst of party-goers, be sure to fill the punch bowl with floating hands made by freezing fruit drink in a plastic glove.

cool ghoul treats

supplies

Clear plastic or latex gloves
Sugar-free flavored fruit drink mix
Gummy worms, optional
Twist ties
Paper towels
Cookie sheet
Scissors

what to do

1 If the gloves have a powdery residue inside, turn them inside out and soak in warm water or wipe with soapy water and rinse. Allow gloves to dry. Or, turn gloves inside out, leaving the powdery side to the outside.

2 Mix up fruit drink (sugar-free liquid freezes better than liquids with sugar) and pour into the gloves. If desired, add gummy worms to the juice before freezing. Add enough drink to fill gloves loosely but not so full that the fingers will not move. Fasten the gloves tightly with a twist tie. Place paper towels on a cookie sheet and lay the hands on the towels. Freeze.

3 When hands are frozen solid, cut off gloves with scissors. Float hands in a bowl of punch.

fun 'n' freaky invites

supplies for the cat invite

Tracing paper
Pencil
Scissors
Marking pens in silver and black
Craft paper in black, yellow, and white
Glue stick
4x5¼-inch brown craft postcard
¾-inch round red sticker

continued on page 126

125

what to do for the cat invite

1 Trace head and face patterns, *opposite,* onto tracing paper and cut out. The silver and black lines will be drawn with marking pens. Trace around head and center eye patterns on black paper, eyes on yellow, and teeth on white. Cut out.

2 Glue black head shape to center of postcard. Add yellow eyes, black pupils, and white teeth. Apply a red sticker to make the nose.

3 Use a black marking pen to draw in teeth lines, stars, dots, and swirls as shown on pattern. Use a silver pen to draw in whiskers and lines in eyes. Color in stars and one tooth. Add silver dots on top of black dots and in the center of swirls.

4 Write party information on back side of card.

supplies for the skeleton invite

Tracing paper
Pencil
Scissors
Craft paper in black, white, orange, and yellow
Marking pens in silver and black
Glue stick
Round reinforcement stickers in yellow, purple, and green
Small round green stickers

what to do for the skeleton invite

1 Trace the patterns, *opposite,* onto tracing paper and cut out. The silver and black lines will be drawn with marking pens. Fold a piece of black paper in half, bringing the short ends together. Trace around the card shape on the folded piece of black paper. Trace around the bow-tie shape on orange and the skeleton head on white. Cut out shapes. Cut a $3\frac{3}{4} \times \frac{5}{8}$-inch strip from yellow paper.

2 Glue the head shape approximately $\frac{1}{4}$ inch from the top of the card. Use the silver pen to draw in the arms and ribs.

3 Add small round and reinforcement stickers to the bow tie as desired. Trim or fold under stickers that hang over the edge of the bow tie. Glue the bow tie to the bottom of the head.

Glue the yellow paper strip to the bottom of the card.

4 Use a black pen to draw in face details and lettering. On the inside, write "And somewhere to go!" with a silver pen. Add the details to the eyes using the silver pen.

5 Write the invitation information on the inside of the card.

supplies for the "come if you dare" invite

$5\frac{1}{2} \times 8\frac{1}{2}$-inch piece of purple paper
Glue stick
$3\frac{3}{4} \times 5$-inch piece of black paper
Computer or magazines to make lettering
Computer paper
Scissors
Black marking pen

what to do for the "come if you dare" invite

1 Fold the purple paper in half, bringing the short ends together. Using the photo on *page 125* as a guide, glue the black piece of paper onto one side of the purple paper at an angle.

2 To make the words, use a computer to print each word in a different font. Make the word "please" approximately $\frac{1}{4}$ inch high. Make the remaining words and exclamation point between $\frac{1}{2}$ and $1\frac{1}{8}$ inches high. If a computer is not available, clip the letters or entire words from magazines. Glue the words in place.

3 Write the party information on the inside of card.

All Dressed Up...

SKELETON INVITE PATTERN

CAT INVITE PATTERN

a friendly fiends' feast

Gather around this enticing table filled with fanciful pumpkins and irresistible fare that will satisfy any goblin's appetite. The menu offers sausage links in cranberry sauce, sticks-and-stones snack mix, cookie wreaths crawling with edible spiders, delicious sandwiches, and a spritzed fruit drink that keeps cold with wiggle worm ice. For dessert try a shrunken head— a caramel apple trimmed with nuts and candies.

bubbling cranberry-sauced links

supplies
1 8-ounce can jellied cranberry sauce
$1/3$ cup catsup
1 tablespoon lemon juice
$1/2$ teaspoon dry mustard
$1/8$ teaspoon allspice
1 5.3-ounce package small fully cooked smoked sausage links

what to do
1 In a medium saucepan, stir together the cranberry sauce, catsup, lemon juice, dry mustard, and allspice. Cook and stir over medium heat until bubbly. Add the sausage links. Cover and cook over medium-low heat about 10 minutes or until heated through, stirring occasionally. Makes 8 servings.
Crockery cooker directions: Combine cranberry sauce, catsup, lemon juice, dry mustard, and allspice in a 1-quart crockery cooker. Stir in the smoked sausage links. Cover and cook for about 2 hours or until heated through.

continued on page 131

129

SHRUNKEN HEADS

shrunken heads

supplies

8 medium apples
8 wood sticks
Butter
1 cup coarsely
   chopped nuts,
   such as pecans,
   walnuts, or
   peanuts
21 ounces (about
   75) vanilla
   caramels or
   chocolate
   caramels,
   unwrapped
3 tablespoons
   water
6 ounces vanilla-
   flavor candy
   coating
2 teaspoons
   shortening
Desired candies
   for decoration,
   such as licorice,
   candy corn,
   gumdrops,
   candy-coated
   chocolate
   pieces, optional
Tubes of writing
   gel decorating
   icing
Canned frosting

what to do

1 Wash and dry apples. Remove stems. Insert one wood stick into the stem end of each apple. Place apples on a buttered baking sheet. Place chopped nuts in a shallow dish; set aside.

2 In a heavy medium saucepan, heat and stir the caramels and water over medium-low heat just until caramels are melted.

3 Dip each apple into hot caramel mixture, spooning caramel evenly over apple. Allow excess caramel to drip off. Briefly set bottoms of apples in chopped nuts. Set apples on prepared baking sheet and let stand about 30 minutes or until firm.

4 In a heavy, small saucepan, heat and stir the vanilla-flavor candy coating and shortening over low heat just until mixture is melted. Holding apples over the saucepan, spoon the melted candy coating evenly over the tops of the caramel-coated apples. Return to baking sheet and let stand about 30 minutes or until firm.

5 Decorate the apples to resemble faces or monsters using desired candies and writing gel. Use writing gel or canned frosting to attach candies to dipped apples. Makes 8 medium apples.

To make ahead: Prepare apples as directed. Cover and chill for up to two days.

DRESSED-UP
PUMPKINS

dressed-up pumpkins

supplies

Buttons
Acrylic gems in a
   variety of colors
   and shapes
Pumpkin
Towel
Thick white crafts
   glue
Ribbon
Purchased hat to
   fit pumpkin
Belt buckle

continued on page 133

SPRITZED FRUIT DRINK
WITH WIGGLE WORM ICE

what to do

1 Using the photograph on *page 131* for ideas, decide arrangement of buttons and gems to make a face on pumpkin. Rest pumpkin on a towel so the side you wish to decorate is facing up. Glue the trims in place. Let the glue dry.

2 Measure a length of ribbon to fit around hat and add 2 inches. Cut ribbon. Weave one end through a belt buckle. Glue above brim. Let dry. Place hat on pumpkin. Glue in place if desired.

spritzed fruit drink with wiggle worm ice

supplies for fruit drink

1 12-ounce can frozen pineapple-orange juice concentrate

1 12-ounce can apricot nectar, chilled

2 12-ounce cans lemon-lime carbonated beverage, chilled

supplies for wiggle worm ice

1 6-ounce can frozen pineapple-orange juice concentrate

Snack-size, self-sealing plastic bags

Chewy, fruit-flavored candy worms

what to do for fruit drink

1 In a small punch bowl, prepare pineapple-orange juice concentrate according to package directions, using cold water. Stir in the apricot nectar. Add the carbonated beverage, stirring gently to mix.

Carefully add the wiggle worm ice.

what to do for wiggle worm ice

1 Prepare one 6-ounce can frozen pineapple-orange juice concentrate. Divide juice equally among six small (snack-size) self-sealing plastic bags. Place several chewy, fruit-flavored worms in each bag. Seal bag. Place bags in the freezer for several hours or until frozen. Remove ice from bags before using. Makes 6 ice pieces.

To make an ice ring, arrange chewy fruit worms in the bottom of a 4-cup ring. Pour juice into mold to almost cover worms. Do not allow the worms to float. Cover and place in freezer for 1 hour or until frozen.

SPIDERY COOKIE WREATHS

spidery cookie wreaths

supplies

¾ cup butter

¾ cup sugar

¼ teaspoon baking powder

1 egg

1 teaspoon vanilla

1¾ cups flour

¼ cup finely chopped pecans or almonds

1 teaspoon grated orange peel

¼ teaspoon orange paste food coloring

1 recipe decorating icing

Decorating bag

continued on page 134

133

Writing tip #2
Red cinnamon candies or miniature candy-coated semisweet chocolate pieces, optional

what to do

1 In a large mixing bowl, beat the butter with an electric mixer on medium to high speed about 30 seconds or until softened. Add the sugar and baking powder. Beat until combined, scraping the sides of the bowl occasionally. Beat in the egg and vanilla. Beat in as much of the flour as you can with the mixer. Using a wooden spoon, stir in remaining flour.

2 Place half of the dough in a small mixing bowl. Stir in the pecans or almonds; set aside. To the remaining dough, knead in the orange peel and food coloring. Cover and chill both portions of dough about 30 minutes or until easy to handle.

3 On a lightly floured surface, shape each dough portion into a 12-inch-long log. Cut each log into twenty-four ½-inch-thick pieces. Roll each piece into a 6-inch-long rope. If necessary, cover and chill ropes for 10 to 15 minutes if soft and difficult to work with. Place a white and an orange rope side by side and twist together 5 or 6 times. Shape into a circle, gently pinching together the ends where they meet. Place on an ungreased cookie sheet. Repeat with remaining dough, leaving 2 inches between cookies. Bake in a 375° oven for 8 to 10 minutes or until edges are light brown. Cool on cookie sheet about 1 minute, then remove and cool thoroughly on a wire rack.

4 Using a decorating bag and writing tip #2, pipe icing into various-size spiders randomly on cookies. If desired, use red cinnamon candies, or candy-coated chocolate pieces for the body of the spider. Use a dab of icing to hold body on cookie. Let cookies stand until icing is set. Makes 24 cookies.

Decorating Icing: In a small mixing bowl, stir together 1 cup sifted powdered sugar and enough milk to make an icing of piping consistency. Tint with desired colors of paste or liquid food coloring. Makes ⅓ cup.

wrapped mummy sandwich loaf

supplies

¾ **cup chopped green or red sweet pepper (1 medium)**
½ **cup chopped carrot**
1 tablespoon butter or margarine
1 cup sliced fresh mushrooms
1 3-ounce package cream cheese or cream cheese with chives
½ **of a 10-ounce package frozen chopped spinach, thawed and well drained**
2 ounces thinly sliced Canadian-style bacon, cooked ham, or pepperoni, chopped (½ cup)

¼ **cup fine dry
bread crumbs**
1 **teaspoon dried
Italian seasoning,
crushed**
1 **16-ounce loaf
frozen white bread
dough, thawed
Milk
Sesame seeds or
grated Parmesan
cheese, optional**

what to do

1 In a large skillet,
cook and stir
sweet pepper and
carrot in hot butter
or margarine for
2 minutes. Add
mushrooms; cook
and stir about
2 minutes more or
until vegetables are
tender. Remove from
heat. Stir in cream
cheese, spinach,
meat, bread
crumbs, and Italian
seasoning.

2 On a lightly
floured surface,
roll dough into a
12×9-inch rectangle.
Carefully transfer
to a greased baking
sheet. Spread the

filling lengthwise in
a 3-inch-wide strip
down the center of
rectangle to within
1 inch of the ends.

3 On both long
sides, make
3-inch cuts from
the edges toward
the center at 1-inch
intervals. Moisten
the end of each
dough strip. Starting
at one end,
alternately fold
opposite strips of
dough at an angle
across filling.
Slightly press
moistened ends
together in center
to seal. Cover and
let rise in a warm
place until nearly
double (about
30 minutes).

4 Lightly brush
loaf with milk.
If desired, sprinkle
with sesame seeds
or Parmesan
cheese. Bake in a
350° oven for
25 to 30 minutes or
until golden brown.
Cool slightly on a
wire rack. Using a

serrated knife, cut
into slices. Makes
12 slices.

sticks-and-stones snack mix

supplies

3 **cups puffed
corn cereal**
2 **cups crispy corn
and rice cereal**
2½ **cups tiny
pretzel sticks**
1½ **cups salted
mixed nuts or
shelled pumpkin
seeds**
3 **tablespoons
butter or
margarine**
1 **tablespoon
Worcestershire
sauce**
1 **to** 1½ **teaspoons
chili powder or
barbecue spice**

½ **to** ¾ **teaspoon
garlic powder**
3 **cups crunchy
cheese-flavor
snacks**

what to do

1 In a 15×11×2-inch
baking pan,
combine the corn
cereal, corn and
rice cereal,
pretzel sticks, and
mixed nuts or
pumpkin seeds.

2 In a small
saucepan, heat
butter or margarine,
Worcestershire
sauce, chili powder
or barbecue spice,
and garlic powder
over low heat until
butter melts. Drizzle
over cereal mixture,
tossing to coat.

3 Bake in a 300°
oven for
30 minutes, stirring
once or twice. Add
cheese-flavored
snacks, tossing to
mix. Spread on foil;
cool. Store in an
airtight container for
up to 5 days. Makes
about 11 cups.

Celebrate Halloween by dressing the tabletop with clever screen place mats and cobweb-etched jars perfect for sweet treats or colorful beverages.

table trims

halloween place mat

supplies
Old place mat
Cloth window
  screen fabric
Scissors
Waxed paper
2 to 3 yards of
  1¼-inch-wide
  ribbon
Thick white crafts
  glue
Narrow rickrack

what to do

1 Use an old place mat as a pattern to cut shape from screen.

2 Place window screen on a piece of waxed paper. Cut ribbon in lengths to fit each edge of mat, cutting corners at an angle for a mitered look. Apply glue to back side of each strip of ribbon and lay ribbon along each edge of window screen mat.

3 Turn window screen over and repeat the process for the back side.

4 On one side of the place mat, glue a continuous length of narrow rickrack to inside edge of ribbon.

eerie etched jar

supplies
Tracing paper
Pencil
Typing paper
Scissors
Pint-size jar with
  wide mouth
Vinegar
Black shiny paint
  pen
Crafts knife; cloth
Glass etching
  cream

what to do

1 Trace the pattern, *right,* and transfer design to strip of paper cut the height of the jar and long enough to wrap around the jar.

2 Wash jar in hot water with vinegar. Let dry.

3 Slip the paper pattern inside the jar with the pattern facing toward the outside of the jar.

4 Use black paint pen to trace the seven spokes of the web. Allow the paint to dry. When dry, add the connecting lines to the spokes of the web. Allow the paint to dry. Use a crafts knife to scrape away unwanted paint.

5 With a cloth dipped in vinegar, remove fingerprints from the sides of the jar.

6 Follow the directions on the jar of the etching cream to apply cream to the entire surface of the jar.

7 Wash away etching cream. Peel off paint pen. Let dry.

SPIDER WEB PATTERN

beanbag toss

Ready...aim...toss! Kids will love to play this party game, adding up points by tossing pumpkin-, ghost-, and cat-shape felt beanbags into the openings in the pumpkin. When not in use, place the pumpkin in the yard for all to see and enjoy.

supplies for pumpkin board

Pencil
4x4-foot $\frac{1}{2}$-inch-thick exterior fir plywood
Jigsaw; sandpaper
Exterior paint in bright orange, dark orange, and black

1x4x30-inch fir (brace)
$1\frac{1}{2}$x$2\frac{1}{2}$-inch butt hinge with screws
16-inch light-duty chain with two $\frac{1}{2}$-inch-long screws to fit
Drill and drill bit
24 inches of No. 9 wire (handle)

supplies for beanbags

(one of each shape)
Tracing paper
Pencil
Two 5-inch squares each of white and orange felt
Two 6-inch squares of black felt
Water-erasable marking pen
Scissors
Small scrap of green calico
Black and white embroidery floss
Needle
Beans or rice
Pinking shears

what to do

1 For the pumpkin board, enlarge the pumpkin pattern, *page 141,* and trace onto sheet of plywood. Cut out with saw. Cut out eyes, nose, and mouth. Sand the edges. Paint the entire pumpkin

dry. Paint the lines around the eyes black and the remaining lines dark orange.

2 Attach the brace to back at top edge using hinge. Screw chain between brace and pumpkin at bottom edge. Drill holes in top of pumpkin 1½ inches from top and 4 inches from sides. Attach wire through holes.

3 For beanbags, enlarge the patterns, *page 140,* onto tracing paper. Transfer each design onto one square of felt (ghost on white, pumpkin on orange, and cat on black) using marking pen. (Note: Do not cut out.) Cut a 1½x2¾-inch rectangle from green calico for the pumpkin stem.

4 Using all six

embroidery floss, and referring to dots on patterns, work black French knots for ghost eyes, white French knots for cat eyes, and black Xs for pumpkin eyes. Work black backstitches for pumpkin smile.

5 For pumpkin stem, fold calico in half crosswise, right sides together, to form a ¾×1⅝-inch rectangle. Using ¼ inch seams, sew short sides. Turn right side out. Press under ¼ inch on raw edge.

6 Place the embroidered square atop unstitched square, wrong sides facing. Pin pumpkin stem to top of pumpkin

on pattern. Stitch along sewing line, leaving opening as indicated by slashes on pattern. Fill bags with beans or rice, then sew openings closed. Cut out ¼ inch from seam using pinking shears.

continued on page 140

FRENCH KNOT (LEFT)

BACKSTITCH (BELOW)

PUMPKIN
PADDLEBALL
PATTERN

BAT
PADDLEBALL
PATTERN

GHOST PADDLEBALL
PATTERN

142

playful paddleballs

Young guests will enjoy playing with (and taking home) these painted Halloween paddleball favors. Make them ahead using the patterns, opposite, or have the kids paint them at the party using their own Halloween designs. The paint dries quickly so the games will be ready to go when the guests start heading for home.

supplies

Acrylic paints in black, white, gray, orange, and yellow
Paintbrush
Purchased paddleballs
Tracing paper
Pencil with round-tip eraser
Transfer paper
Silver marking pen

what to do

1 Paint the background color of the design on the entire back of the paddle and sides. Paint the background for the ghost white, the pumpkin orange, and the bats gray. Let the paint dry.

2 Trace the desired patterns, *opposite.* Use transfer paper to transfer the details to the painted side of the paddleball. Paint in the details using the patterns as a guide. Let the paint dry. To make eyes on the bats, dip the eraser end of a pencil or the handle end of a paintbrush into white paint and dot onto the heads of the bats. Let the paint dry. Add smaller black dots in the center of each eye. Let the paint dry.

3 Use a silver marking pen to add dotted-line swirls to the bat paddleball board.

4 Paint the attached balls using the photograph, *right,* for inspiration. Let the paint dry.

143

index

Designers
Susan M. Banker
Donna Chesnut
Carol Field Dahlstrom
Phyllis Dobbs
Phyllis Dunstan
Margaret Sindelar
Barb Smith
Alice Wetzel